"Leonydus expertly lays out why parents raising children in the woke world take the path of least resistance and the danger of it."

—**Leland Vittert,** anchor at NewsNation

"*Raising Victims* is a scathing repudiation of both Critical Race Theory and the prevailing focus on race in the ethos of Western civilization. Part Sheena Mason's *Theory of Racelessness*, part Thomas Sowell's *Discrimination and Disparities*—Johnson makes the case in his unique voice using history, personal stories, and pop culture references to highlight the flaws in the theory and the overall acceptance of progressive racism. Not content with only pointing out problems, he offers an alternative solution to our culture problems that go beyond the toxic, hyper-racial approach that has driven the country race-crazy."

—**Charles Love,** scholar with 1776 Unites, cohost of *Cut the Bull Podcast*, and author of *Race Crazy: BLM, 1619, and the Progressive Racism Movement*

"Leonydus Johnson smashes the notion that lies become truth simply because a large segment of society believes them or says otherwise. Our culture has been run over by a group of elitists who make it easier to be a victim than a victor. In *Raising Victims*, Leonydus accurately details their ludicrous reasoning while exposing the real agenda."

—**Tom Roten,** host of *The Tom Roten Morning Show*

Raising Victims

RAISING VICTIMS

THE PERNICIOUS RISE OF CRITICAL RACE THEORY

LEONYDUS JOHNSON

SALEM
BOOKS

an imprint of Regnery Publishing
Washington, D.C.

Salem Books™ is a trademark of Salem Communications Holding Corporation.
Regnery® and its colophon is a registered trademark of Salem Communications Holding Corporation.
Cataloging-in-Publication data on file with the Library of Congress.

ISBN: 978-1-68451-377-2
eISBN: 978-1-68451-397-0

Library of Congress Control Number: 2022949156

Published in the United States by
Salem Books
An Imprint of Regnery Publishing
A Division of Salem Media Group
Washington, D.C.
www.SalemBooks.com

Manufactured in the United States of America

10 9 8 7 6 5 4 3 2 1

Books are available in quantity for promotional or premium use. For information on discounts and terms, please visit our website: www.SalemBooks.com.

CONTENTS

CHAPTER 1

What Is Critical Race Theory?

*We are among the biggest fools in history if we keep on
paying people to make us hate each other.*

—Thomas Sowell

By now, most Americans have at least heard of the term "Critical Race Theory." It is an ideology that was developed in the late 1970s and throughout the 80s, but it has only recently risen to national prominence, finding its way into all levels of political debates, news stories and think pieces, and our everyday conversations. Despite this increased awareness, a definition for Critical Race Theory seems to be somewhat elusive, even among those who claim to support it. This definitional haziness has been used as a strategic tool to outright dismiss any concerns from parents about the race-centric curricula being imposed on their children in public schools, concerns from employees about race-centric training sessions being required in the workplace, or concerns from citizens about race-centric policies being enacted by the government. The simple refrain is, "That isn't Critical Race Theory."

Then what exactly *is* Critical Race Theory (CRT)? While its opponents vehemently denounce it as blatant racism disguised in costumes like diversity, equity, and inclusion (DEI) initiatives, its supporters insist it is nothing more than an academic tool of analysis found only in law schools. Who is correct?

In *Critical Race Theory: An Introduction*, one of the founders of the ideology, Richard Delgado, tells us explicitly what it is, writing:

> The critical race theory (CRT) movement is a collection of activists and scholars engaged in studying and transforming the relationship among race, racism, and power. The movement considers many of the same issues that conventional civil rights and ethnic studies discourses take up but places them in a broader perspective that includes economics, history, setting, group and self-interest, and emotions and the unconscious. Unlike traditional civil rights discourse, which stresses incrementalism and step-by-step progress, critical race theory questions the very foundations of the liberal order, including equality theory, legal reasoning, Enlightenment rationalism, and neutral principles of constitutional law.[1]

In essence, CRT is an ideology embraced by race activists that operates from the foundational assumption that racism is endemic in our country; that it is deeply ingrained in all of our institutions; that it is intertwined into the very fabric of our society; that concepts such as equality, neutral principles of law, and liberalism (i.e., individual rights, liberty, consent of the governed, etc.) are its natural enemies; and that this must be rectified, not through incrementalism, but through revolution. The belief is that racism is so pervasive that it has embedded itself into the normal, everyday operations of our lives to the point of invisibility. Racial disparities viewed through the lens of CRT are automatically attributed to racism even if no overtly racist acts are apparent. White people are said to benefit from a system of white supremacy whether they know it or not. Non-white people are likewise oppressed by this same system whether they know it or not. In this view, the fundamental operation of the system itself automatically perpetuates racism and disparate outcomes among racial groups. These are the basic tenets of Critical Race Theory.

It should be clear how insidious such an ideology can be. It completely removes the agency of the individual and claims that outcomes are wholly dependent on invisible systems—systems that were apparently built to perpetually sustain white supremacy, even if no actual white supremacists operate within it.

The notion is ridiculous on its face. Systems are not racist. People are. Systems do not engage in discriminatory behavior. People do. It is a nonsensical proposition that a system can somehow be created to covertly perpetuate racist bigotry and discrimination without the awareness or knowledge of its participants. Imagine that, under Jim Crow, a restaurant enforces segregation and refuses to serve black customers or makes them sit in a separate area from the white customers. We might say that Jim Crow and the subsequent policies of this restaurant were examples of systemic racism. However, the discriminatory actions do not actually happen unless individuals consciously engage in the behavior to enforce segregation. They wouldn't do it unconsciously. They wouldn't do it while failing to recognize that their behavior was discriminatory and racially motivated. They wouldn't be surprised to find out that the system had different rules for different people based on race.

In other words, the system cannot segregate or engage in racism on its own. In fact, there were many instances of companies during the Jim Crow era defying segregation laws because they had economic incentives to do so. If the system was inherently racist, they wouldn't have been able to do that. Racism doesn't just happen invisibly and without the conscious awareness of those involved. To say otherwise is to substantially diminish the essence and implications of the word "racism" to the point where it becomes meaningless.

Claims of racist systems are nothing more than a convenient boogeyman one can draw from in order to explain disparities in outcomes without laying agency and responsibility at the feet of the individual. Black people are disproportionately shot by police? Policing must be racist. Black actors aren't nominated for at least half of the Academy Awards? The Academy must be racist. Black people struggle with math? Math must be racist. This is CRT's answer for every racial disparity. There is no need to examine crime rates, quality of acting work, or time spent on math homework. In the world of Critical Race Theory, the culprit is always the "system," and the only variable that truly matters is race.

Ibram X. Kendi, a professor at Boston University and the face of the so-called "antiracism" movement, has stated explicitly that racial disparities in a given system are evidence that the system is racist. He has also said that the only remedy for past discrimination is present discrimination, and that the only remedy for present discrimination is future discrimination—meaning that the tables must be turned, and white people must now become and remain the victims of discrimination in order to make up for past discrimination against black people. It is incredible that anyone treats these ideas with even a modicum of seriousness. The endorsement of open racism aside, the idea that disparities cannot possibly exist between two groups without the presence of bias is just nonsense. If it's foolish to expect equal outcomes between individuals (and it is), then it is foolish to expect equal outcomes between groups of individuals. To quote Dr. Thomas Sowell, "A man isn't even equal to himself on different days."[2] It makes little sense to expect even people who embrace the same culture, the same beliefs, and the same values to have equal outcomes, including children who grow up in the same household with the same parents. So how much less sensible is it to expect equal outcomes among people who engage in disparate cultures, beliefs, and values?

For example, when a given group has a disproportionate number of individuals embracing a degenerate culture of violence and criminality when compared to another group, why would it be surprising to find the first group is disproportionately represented in police encounters, arrests, and police shootings? Are we to conclude that law enforcement officers are misandrists, since the vast majority of people arrested and killed by police are men? Or are there other variables that might explain the disparity? Making it about race distorts the real problem: the individuals who are engaged in the degenerate behaviors and degenerate cultures, which has little to do with anyone else, regardless of skin color. Blaming disparities on racism is pure intellectual dishonesty.

"Whiteness"

What is also often forgotten (or shall we say, ignored) in these discussions is that there are often more significant intragroup disparities than intergroup disparities. If disparities automatically equal bias, then how do we explain why black people who engage in different cultural behaviors experience significantly different outcomes? What explains the disparity between a wealthy black person and an impoverished black person? Is it bias? Of course, CRT advocates would blame such disparities on white supremacy anyway and claim that black people who experience more positive outcomes do so because they engage in "white behaviors" or align themselves closely with "whiteness." According to this view, black people only manage to succeed in this system of white supremacy because they "act white," while those who "act black" remain eternally under the boot of white oppression. This is what this ideology promotes. I have personally been told that I benefit from white privilege because of my "white-normative" behavior. Such arguments, of course, ironically undermine the claims of systemic racism, because if this racism can be so easily defeated by simply modifying one's behavior, then the problem clearly isn't racism. These ridiculous accusations would be comical if the ideology weren't so pervasive.

So what exactly are these "white behaviors"? According to the Smithsonian's National Museum of African-American History and Culture, white behaviors and white culture include such things as rugged individualism; the nuclear family; emphasis on the scientific method; Western-focused history; having a strong work ethic; Christianity; respecting authority; valuing ownership of goods, space, and property; beauty standards; Christian holidays; our traditional definition of justice; a competitive spirit; proper English grammar; and politeness.[3] How is it that more people are not insulted by these assertions? To claim that concepts like politeness, respect, and work ethic are traits of "whiteness" is to imply that impoliteness, disrespect, and laziness are the traits of non-whiteness. If you were looking for racism, there it is.

Along with this, there is also a sense among those who follow the ideas of Critical Race Theory that the black people who deviate from the expectations of "blackness" (whatever that means) are to be considered white, or at least purveyors of white supremacy. This brings to mind an exchange between *Washington Post* reporter Eugene Scott and Nikole Hannah-Jones, the founder of the historically illiterate 1619 Project. Scott said, "These days, I am reminded quite often that you do not have to be white to support white supremacy," to which Jones responded,

Also, whiteness is not static, and it is expandable when necessary. A lot of folks we don't think of as white think of themselves as white because the lines have never been entirely clear. That's the beauty of white supremacy—it is extremely adaptable.[4]

This is the epitome of psychological projection. Scott lays the groundwork by claiming non-whites can support white supremacy and Jones gives the game away by announcing that the concept of white supremacy is malleable. This means that, for advocates of Critical Race Theory, "whiteness" and "white supremacy" are quite literally whatever they say it is, and the definitions remain fluid and dynamic, ready to serve whatever purpose they need it to.

Hannah-Jones has also been known to make a distinction between those who are physically black and those who are "politically black" to make this same point. In other words, you can only truly be black if you agree with her and her ideology. Otherwise, you support white supremacy. Genius. Just make white supremacy mean whatever you want it to mean, and then you can accuse anybody you want to of supporting it. Of course, if it means supporting punctuality, work ethic, individualism, or proper grammar, then you will find plenty of non-white people who support white supremacy. If it means opposing progressivism, the 1619 Project, Critical Race Theory, or just the general idea that black people are oppressed in America, then go ahead and sign me up as a non-politically black white supremacist.

But this is how CRT justifies itself. The claim that there are systems of white supremacy cannot be refuted if the racism in the system is invisible and the definition of white supremacy is fluid and based on whatever is needed in the moment. I am reminded of the teenager who claims he has a girlfriend but when pressed about her identity, announces that you wouldn't know her anyway and she goes to another school.

Anti-Colorblindness and Ethnic Gnosticism

Critical Race Theory also rejects the idea of colorblindness and treating everyone equally regardless of their race. It dismisses the oft-referenced line of Dr. Martin Luther King's "I Have a Dream" speech, in which he proclaimed that he looked forward to a day where his children would be judged, not by the color of their skin, but by the content of their character. CRT advocates believe that such a view is actually oppressive. They believe that if everyone were to be treated the same, and if race were essentially ignored, then the system of white supremacy would run unchecked, allocating privilege and status to white people while grinding non-white people into the ground under its heel. They believe that race must be placed at the forefront of policy- and decision-making in order to manipulate outcomes.

They believe in a concept that one of the progenitors of CRT, Harvard Law professor Derrick Bell, called "Interest Convergence," which essentially means that white people control the levers of power and never do anything that will benefit black people unless it also benefits themselves. In other words, black people never make any gains or receive any benefit in society unless their interests and the interests of white people converge. Bell argued, for example, that the U.S. Supreme Court only ruled that racially segregating schoolchildren is unconstitutional in *Brown v. Board of Education* (1954) because it was in the interest of white people to elevate their image on the world stage during the Cold War.

What Bell and others fail to understand is that people, in general, operate in self-interest regardless of race. Everyone does. The entire idea of commerce in a free market is dependent on the fact that people act in their own self-interest and that they choose to do business with each other when those interests converge. This is true on the individual level, but the government never does anything for anyone, regardless of race, unless it is in the government's best interest and helps it maintain or grow its power. If it is in the government's interest to deny you your rights and it can get away with it, it will do so. We saw that clearly during the COVID-19 pandemic. The state is the problem. It always has been. That has nothing to do with race.

CRT advocates also do not believe in equal opportunity, only in equal results. As such, they believe that if they control the levers of power, they can create equal outcomes and will not have to rely on interest convergence. They are antagonistic toward any concept of equal treatment—even the idea of rights—themselves. They believe, again, that these things only benefit white people while oppressing non-white people. They believe concepts like "free speech" are mechanisms of marginalization: that speech is only free for white people who use their speech to advance their own power and further marginalize minority groups. They maintain that dismissing the idea of positive rights (i.e., the right *to* something, such as housing) in favor of negative rights (the right to be free *from* something, such as coercion) is nothing more than yet another form of oppression and a product of a white-dominated culture. They believe in standpoint epistemology—the idea that racial minorities have significantly more authority to understand and speak on supposed racial oppression due to their position as the oppressed while others (white people) do not. They reject the concept of objectivity and embrace the pseudo-reality of "lived experience" and "my truth" over empirical evidence and *the* truth. They believe in equity, which means sacrificing true equality in pursuit of equal outcomes. They believe they can and should take from the "haves" according to their perceived privilege and give to the "have nots" according to their perceived marginalization. CRT is merely repackaged Marxism, with race replacing class (more on that in Chapter Twelve).

This is the game that is being played by Critical Race Theory activists. They believe the entire structure of our society is corrupted with racism and racial oppression. And not only is this apparent oppression invisible, but it can only be recognized, understood, and explained by non-white people who adhere to the CRT ideology and who have special white supremacy decoder rings. Everyone else is, therefore, oblivious and unable to understand the experiences of those who suffer under the hand of white supremacy. They believe that white people cannot possibly know what it is like to be black in America, as their own experiences are skewed by the lens of white privilege. Theologian and author Voddie Baucham calls this "ethnic gnosticism": the concepts of race and racism are treated as if racial minorities, and specifically black people, live some sort of mystical, esoteric existence that cannot possibly be grasped by anyone with a different skin color. Therefore, since you as a white person cannot possibly understand what it is like to be black, you are not allowed to have any opinions pertaining to race. This would also mean that my white family members and I somehow have much less in common and understand each other much less than I and some stranger in a random city across the country who happens to be black would.

In its stated quest to eradicate racism, CRT manipulatively places race at the forefront of everything and proclaims it to be the most powerful and important variable of a person's identity. It claims to be fighting white supremacy while, ironically, making the exact same types of racial arguments that white supremacists have made.

CRT is an ideology that latches onto the past and refuses to let go, dragging as much of that past as it can into the present for the purpose of emotional manipulation. It is an ideology that believes the son remains guilty of his father's sins. It is an ideology that embraces the erroneous and damaging assumption that disparities automatically equal bias, that skin color confers privilege (or lack thereof), and that this all must be dismantled at the institutional level. It is a conspiracy theory that removes all agency from non-white people and places the blame for all negative or disparate outcomes of non-white individuals onto the specter of white supremacy.

This, in turn, encourages the bigotry of low expectations through which non-white people are not held to the same standards as their white counterparts and are given special accommodations and considerations in order to be "equal." This is why, in school systems, we see advanced-placement classes and standardized testing discontinued. Grading systems are altered or abolished. Grammar requirements are loosened. White children are taught that they must deconstruct their whiteness and recognize their privilege, while non-white students are taught that they are inherently victims of a hateful and bigoted system. In corporate settings, white employees are forced to undergo racial sensitivity training and listen to lectures from so-called diversity consultants on how racist they are and how they must "be less white." In Hollywood, there are demands for more non-white actors to be cast regardless of whether they are a good fit for the role and that they win more awards whether they deserve them or not—all while propaganda is continually infused into films and TV shows that promote the notion of rampant racism against minorities as well as the desirability and virtue of white guilt.

Professional sports leagues are receiving demands for more black coaches while ignoring the disproportionate number of black players. People like Colin Kaepernick claim that NFL players, who make millions of dollars to play a game, are the equivalent of slaves in a slave auction. We see victimhood messaging on helmets and sidelines about how significant a problem racism is in America, and athletes kneeling during the national anthem in some contrived sense of solidarity with those who suffer the horrors of being black in America. And no white person is ever allowed to protest any of it because they, in their "whiteness," cannot possibly comprehend the horrific experience of living as a black person in the irredeemably racist United States of America.

This is Critical Race Theory at its root. It is the belief that racism is everywhere, at all times, regardless of evidence; that non-white people must be given special attention and accommodations to overcome it; that only non-white people (with the "correct" political views) are in a position to define it; that colorblindness and treating everyone equally only perpetuates it; and that our institutions must be reformed or ultimately destroyed because of it.

St. George in Retirement Syndrome

Critical Race Theory is an ideology that promotes blatant racism, and it was born of a need for its founders to justify their own importance. The founders claim that CRT was developed because the civil rights movement had "stalled out." In reality, it was created because the civil rights movement had largely accomplished its purpose, so the people whose identities were wrapped up in social justice and racial victimhood needed new monsters to fight. What better way to do that than to claim that the overt racism of the past had been driven underground and now covertly and invisibly continues its schemes of white dominance behind the curtains of all of our institutions? What better way to maintain your sense of purpose than to promote an ideology of demagoguery, feeding on hatred and resentment, clinging to grievance and vengefulness, and heralding yourself as the savior?

Political philosopher Kenneth Minogue coined a concept known as "St. George in Retirement Syndrome." It is presented in the form of an allegory, telling the story of a valiant dragon slayer named St. George, who kills all the dragons in the land. Once he has slain all the dragons, he goes home and relaxes, enjoying his retirement.

However, before long he begins to experience an identity crisis. His entire life has revolved around slaying dragons, and now all the dragons are gone. He no longer feels like he has any purpose. As luck would have it, he looks out the window and what does he see? A dragon! He grabs his sword and shield and rushes out to slay the horrid beast. Suddenly he is surrounded. There are dragons every- where! Big dragons, small dragons, dragons with antlers, dragons that bark, dragons that quack, even dragons that pretend to be villagers. St. George heroically slays them all. Eventually he is seen swinging his sword at the empty air itself, proclaiming it to be the biggest, fiercest dragon of all.[5]

I find this allegory to be a spectacular representation of what Critical Race Theory is. There was, indeed, a time when the real dragons of widespread racial oppression existed in this country. There was a time when we needed those dragon slayers, who would valiantly go to battle and kill these terrible monsters. But once the dragons were slain, what were those who had rooted their identity in slaying them supposed to do now? What does a dragon slayer do when all the dragons are gone? The solution was to begin seeing dragons everywhere.

This is now the claim: dragons are all around us. Even when we can't see them, they are there. We must all be aware of these dragons and actively work to destroy them in every aspect of our lives. If you are not a dragon slayer, you are not gifted with the insight necessary to see these dragons—but you must never question their existence. We must trust what we are told, just accept that they truly are perva- sive, that only the dragon slayers are able to see them, and only the dragon slayers can tell us how they must be destroyed. You need to just shut up and be an ally, reflect on your flaws, and figure out how you personally are hindering the dragon slayers and allowing these dragons to continue to terrorize the countryside.

With all this in mind, it seems extremely silly to claim that such an ideology would be restricted only to law schools. How could it be? CRT proclaims that the dragon of racism is all around us, inherent in our very way of life, and that it requires active deconstruction. Its founders insist that it has both an academic and an activist component, that it is a tool for activism and social change, and that movements like Black Lives Matter, antiracism, and DEI are vehicles for CRT ideology. Are we supposed to believe that these people are not pursuing this anywhere except for 8:00 a.m. classes at Yale? Of course not. Clearly, it is not restricted to law schools. The founders of CRT even openly admit that it has expanded to other areas of education, that it has branched off into LGBT issues, Asian-American issues, and Muslim-American issues, and that its principles are being applied in all manners of ways—not only in this country, but all over the world. DEI programs, cultural sensitivity, racial sensitivity—all of these are used as euphemisms for the principles of CRT, none of which have anything to do with education and everything to do with implementation. Why obfuscate these things?

Word Games

Obfuscation is a recognizable pattern within progressivism. The intentional manipulation of words and definitions is a way for people to try to command the narrative, confuse and manipulate others, and to seize and hold power. For example, they say racism cannot possibly be committed by black people (well, politically black people, anyway) because racism requires power. Once you set aside the false claim that black people do not have power in America, it becomes clear that this is a nonsensical proposition meant to excuse the racist behavior of non-white people and to attach the shame of racism solely to white people. There is no other reason to try to shift that definition.

This kind of language manipulation is not exclusive to Critical Race Theory, either. We see it with issues like gender ideology, sexuality, and abortion as well—in fact, in any sociopolitical issue influenced by progressivism, we will inevitably see manipulation of language. The definitions of "man" and "woman" have become fluid. We now must contend with gobbledygook terms such as "birthing people" or "people who menstruate." We must be open and accepting of "pansexuals" and "homoflexibles." What is a human being? What does the word "life" mean? None of these definitions are static in progressivism. The sands shift with every change of topic. If we are just discussing pregnancy, then we must use the term "birthing people," because leftists claim men can get pregnant, too. If we're talking about abortion, all of a sudden men aren't allowed to have an opinion because they can't get pregnant anymore. Who qualifies as a "man" or "woman" is wholly dependent on the political context of the conversation. The most politically advantageous definition is the one that will be used in the given moment—and it doesn't matter if it directly contradicts the other definition the speaker was using five minutes ago.

This is often the key for Critical Race Theory, and it is the only way it can stand up to scrutiny. Any criticism is deflected with a changing definition of what Critical Race Theory actually is or what its terms mean. Hostility toward free speech, being suspicious of the idea of rights, opposing the concept of objectivity, and decrying the true meaning of liberalism are all tenets of CRT, but CRT advocates will accuse you of fabricating what it stands for when you point these things out. They will try to claim that Ibram X. Kendi and Robin DiAngelo (the author of *White Fragility*) have nothing to do with Critical Race Theory, since they did not go to law school—as if that is somehow the requirement to be a CRT activist. It is a constant motte-and-bailey fallacy, through which they embrace extreme ideas (the bailey) and then retreat to more acceptable ideas (the motte) and pretend that's the entirety of their position. This is why when the extreme elements of CRT are challenged, particularly in schools, its proponents will retreat to the motte and respond by saying that all they want to do is teach history. This is intentional manipulation.

In reality, CRT is nothing more than racist pseudoscience. It is Marxism with race replacing class. It is radicalized activism set in universities and public schools to manipulate and indoctrinate students into seeing the world and each other through a toxic, racialized, victim/oppressor lens. It is a vehicle for racial division and segregation. It is a tool for emotional manipulation. It is an ideology of narcissism and ingratitude. It is evil parading as virtue. It is the very monster that it claims to be fighting against. It is the antithesis of a colorblind, post-racial society or any semblance of what is required to move toward one.

Critical Race Theory is not an academic discipline. It is a worldview. It is a belief system. It is an extremist religion. It is a racialized distortion filter through which one views reality and truth and comes away with lies. It is a commandment to spread the gospel of racial grievance and victimhood. It is racism pretending to eradicate racism.

We must see through the word games, recognize CRT for what it is, and tear it down. For anyone who wishes to see the wounds of our past healed, to see true unity in our nation, and to see America finally progress past race and racism in the next generations, Critical Race Theory must be thoroughly and utterly rejected.

We cannot allow ourselves to raise our children to be victims.

CHAPTER 2

Münchausen's by Proxy

They say the truth hurts, but the only thing the truth hurts are illusions.

—Julie Gregory

I have often mused that the thought and behavioral patterns within certain ideologies like Critical Race Theory, along with Kendi's antiracism movement and groups like Black Lives Matter, resemble personality disorders. We see endless examples of paranoia, hostile attribution bias, reality distortion, learned helplessness, and of course, victim mentality. And when this broken way of viewing the world is imposed on children, it is not unlike Münchausen's by Proxy.

Münchausen's Syndrome by Proxy (which has since been renamed Factitious Disorder Imposed on Another) is a mental illness wherein a person, typically a caregiver, claims that another person is ill when they are not—or worse, the caregiver actually induces illness or disability in the other person—so that the caregiver can gain attention and sympathy. Julie Gregory, in her memoir *Sickened: The True Story of a Lost Childhood*, details her experience with Münchausen's by Proxy: her mother would alter her diet, give her all kinds of different medications she was not prescribed, and even have her eat things like

17

matches in order to make her sick.[1] As an innocent child, Julie was not able to understand what was going on and did not recognize until much later that she wasn't actually sick, but that her mother was abusing her. Other people in her life did not realize she was being abused and assumed her mother was telling the truth about her supposed illnesses. How could a parent make a child and others believe that child is sick? It is clearly despicable behavior. So why do we tolerate it when it comes to race?

When adults infuse ideas of racial victimhood into their children's minds, teach them to fear the police, that other people are out to get them, and that all negative interactions are due to people hating them because of their skin color, is that behavior truly different from what Julie Gregory's mother did? When adults teach children that their skin color makes them an oppressor, that they have unearned privilege due to their race, that unless they learn to deconstruct their race, they are participating in a system that intentionally hurts people, that something is inherently wrong with them because of their skin color and that they must actively work to resolve it—is that truly different from what Julie Gregory's mother did?

Children all over the country, regardless of race, are being taught that they are sick, that something is wrong with them, and that something is wrong with the world they interact with. Adults are teaching innocent children to be afraid, to be paranoid, to feel guilt for things they didn't do, and to feel wronged by things they didn't experience. They are being taught to view the ups and downs of life and their normal, everyday interactions through a filter of racial distortion, warping their perception of reality into a grotesque imitation of itself.

To these adults, our entire society is sick and has been throughout all of history. White people are sick and intent on expunging black people. Black people are sick because white people have oppressed them and made them sick, and they will continue to be sick until white people allow society to distribute the medicine equally. These are fabricated symptoms of a false illness.

Why would you ever want to impose that on children? Even when a child is truly ill, why would you want him to center his identity around that illness? Why would you want to instill feelings of victim-hood or guilt into them over it? That is the complete opposite of what a loving parent or a compassionate adult would ever do in such a scenario. Even in the face of a real disease, children should be pro-tected, reassured of their resilience, made to feel hopeful and opti-mistic, and encouraged to be brave and strong and to be an overcomer, not a helpless victim. Even in the face of a real disease, children should be embraced and loved for who they are, not made to feel guilt for something they didn't do and are not responsible for. Even in the face of a real disease, children should not be used as pawns to further some political cause. If all of this is true for a real disease, how much more so when we are dealing with a false one?

Cultural Münchausen's

Children have been the main target of progressive ideology, including Critical Race Theory, for a few reasons. One, like Münchausen's, is to garner attention and sympathy for the people spreading the falsehood. It is emotional manipulation of the masses. Another reason is to mold the future of progressivism through indoctrination of the next generation—an effective way to transform an entire culture. Vladimir Lenin once said, "Give me four years to teach the children, and the seed I have sown will never be uprooted."[2] This has been the out-spoken strategy of progressive leaders and activists for quite some time. They have been intent on capturing our cultural institutions and using them to promote progressive ideology with a particular focus on children. They have done this in public schools, with children's literature, with children's theatre, and with children's television shows and films, etc. They are dedicated to infusing these ideas into the everyday lives of children as much as possible, even if they need to circumvent parents to do it, so that when these kids grow up, they will effectively be foot soldiers for the progressive cause. It is cultural Münchausen's.

While many parents buy into progressive ideology and instill it into their children, many clearly do not—but that does not stop the activists. There is a sentiment among many progressives, particularly those who work in education, that children do not actually belong to their parents; they belong to the system. They belong to the community. Parents are only there as some kind of secondary facilitator of a child's development, while teachers and administrators are the true parents. Disney executives and animators are the true parents. People with the "correct" ideology are the true parents. They are the ones who should raise the children, who will mold and shape them, and who will align them with this "correct" ideology and moral compass, while the parents are merely another obstacle to be overcome in the system of oppression. If the parents object—or worse, if they actively move against progressive ideology—these beings of moral superiority will decide that the parents are dangerous and the child must be turned against them.

There are countless incidents of teachers outright admitting to teaching race-centric lessons to students behind their parents' backs. There are videos of Disney executives discussing how to infuse progressive ideology into films in order to secretly influence the children who watch them. They do this proudly. It seems they believe it is their righteous duty to step in and be the "true" parents of these children and rescue them from their bigoted families.

During the COVID-19 pandemic, when schools were shut down and remote learning was widespread, parents began to become aware of just how much indoctrination was going on in their children's classrooms. As a result, they began to push back. Teachers around the country then began to complain about being undermined by these supposedly bigoted parents and openly contemplated strategies to teach their students via Zoom without the parents in the room and without the parents' knowledge of what was being taught. Attempts to provide transparency for parents about curricula and lesson plans were vehemently rejected and mocked. Parents were silenced and dismissed. They were even labeled "domestic terrorists" by teachers' unions and the federal government. The belief was that as long as their children were in public schools, their kids belonged to the government. These teachers and administrators, along with teachers' unions and politicians, were essentially saying that when it comes to public school, parents have no power, and what their children learn is completely up to those teachers, administrators, unions, and politicians. They told parents to their faces that they do not have the right to control what their children are taught—and that if they want control, they should homeschool their kids or send them to private school. (Which is actually not bad advice, given the state of public schools.)

In October 2021, the *Washington Post* published an op-ed by Jack Schneider and Jennifer Berkshire titled, "Parents Claim They Have the Right to Shape Their Kids' School Curriculum. They Don't."[3] The authors stated outright that if parents want control over their children's education, they "can opt out of the public system if they wish and pay to send their children to private or religious schools." They brazenly claimed that "to turn over all decisions to parents . . . would risk inhibiting the ability of young people to think independently" and that the push for parental rights and opposition to Critical Race Theory in particular is nothing more than a GOP conspiracy to "stoke white grievance." Not only did these writers decide to promote the idea that parents do not and should not have power to control what their children are learning in public schools, but also suggested that those parents are motivated by racism. This op-ed was praised by many in the sphere of public education, including American Federation of Teachers President Randi Weingarten.[4] The AFT is one of the largest teachers unions in the country.

Additionally, teachers unions and the Democrat politicians with whom they are always allied have heavily opposed bills seeking to provide the kind of transparency in curricula that allow parents to know exactly what their children are being taught. They have claimed that such bills would lead to censorship and were intended to keep children from learning about things like racism. Once again, Weingarten and the AFT emerged in the center of this debate, claiming that such bills are not needed because "good schools and good school districts have always had curriculum transparency."[5] One must ask: if this is the case, then why would the union oppose a bill to provide it?

Take a moment to consider the implications of all this: The claims are that government employees tasked with educating children should have the power to tell the people who foot the bill—the people they essentially work for—that they have absolutely no power, authority, or input in what goes on in that institution or to what their own children are exposed. They say parents should have no right to even see the curricula and lesson plans, let alone any input concerning what goes into them. How is that acceptable? Imagine you hired a babysitter whom you later suspect of abusing your children—but that babysitter insists you have no right to tell her how to babysit or to know anything about what she does with your kids when you aren't home. That would be understandably shocking, and that babysitter would almost certainly be fired on the spot and potentially arrested. Why do we treat the government differently?

We shouldn't. But this has become the nature of the public school system, and many people tolerate it. I should add that I recognize that there are many wonderful teachers out there who do exemplary work, and this problem clearly does not describe all educators. However, the problem is still pervasive, and it continues to spread. The ideological poison seems to be so entrenched that it is not entirely clear how public schooling can be salvaged. The only real solution is to get children out of that environment completely, either by providing options that force schools to compete for student dollars, or by homeschooling.

The Fallacy of Race

My wife and I pulled our children out of public school around the time the COVID lockdowns were happening and decided to take full control of their education. Thankfully, we live in a relatively conservative area of southern Ohio, and the madness of progressive ideology was not quite on the level of a school in New York City or Portland, but we should recognize that not even conservative areas are safe from the creep of this ideology and its accompanying Münchausen's by Proxy. DEI initiatives that are commonplace in hiring practices, middle school students announcing that they are pansexual, young girls deciding they are now boys—there is no escaping it except through homeschooling.

We are intent on raising our kids largely outside a racial framework, and homeschooling has helped us do that. My children currently have no racial identity, and we would like to keep it that way for as long as possible. People often ask me how we handle racial issues in our house, and the simple answer is that we don't use racial identity at all, nor do we want to treat skin color as being central to who we are. My kids are completely removed from that. They recognize differences between themselves and other kids, of course, but the importance they place on those differences is negligible.

For instance, my oldest son is dark-skinned with black hair, while my younger son has much lighter skin and blonde hair. My two daughters both have lighter skin with light brown hair. We used to joke that if you lined them all up by age, it would look like a printer was running out of ink. One of my daughters even has blue eyes, while the others' eyes are brown. These differences aren't ignored. They are well aware of these differences. But they see them as inconsequential. They see them as unique to the individual person, and it has no effect on how they treat each other. There is no scale of brotherhood or sisterhood based on skin, hair, or eye color. It is the same with their friends, most of whom are white. It is the same with their entire family on their mom's side, nearly all of whom are white. It isn't a topic of discussion or something they dwell on. They don't spend their days thinking about it or filtering all their experiences through it. It quite literally does not matter. They see these people as their family and as their friends. That's it. There is nothing more to it. They are unique individuals, and they see others as unique individuals.

We don't put much weight on ancestral heritage, either. My wife's ancestry is mixed. Her mother would be considered white and her father would be considered black, but each of them have their own heavily mixed ancestries. My own ancestry is also mixed, including a hodgepodge of people from various countries and cultures. As a result, my children have family members who span the entire spectrum of melanin variation. It seems foolish to teach them that they should be attached to some family members but not others based on race, or that they share an ancestral bond with some family members but not others. It would be asinine to teach them that they are black and therefore victims, or to teach them that they are white and therefore oppressors. It would be foolish to teach them that they must cling to either identity or feel some kind of kinship with strangers who share it—or worse, that they should harbor hostility and suspicion toward those who do not.

We teach our children to view people as people, not as members of racial groups. We have discussed how other people view skin color and race as very important, and that they will attempt to get everyone else to see them that way—but we teach them to reject such distorted ways of seeing the world.

Recently, I was in Athens, Ohio, with my eleven-year-old son, and we saw some "Black Lives Matter" graffiti sprayed all over the sidewalk and some of the buildings. He asked me what it meant. We talked about the fallacy of race, the Black Lives Matter movement, and how there are people who feel skin color is the most important thing about who they are and believe people with darker skin are constantly treated badly in America. He just shrugged his shoulders and said, "That's dumb." (I agree, son. I agree.)

It isn't that we pretend racism doesn't exist. When my kids were still in public school, a little girl who liked my son suddenly decided to stop talking to him. My wife and I didn't think much of it at the time because they were kids in elementary school and far too young to be thinking about boyfriends and girlfriends. But we later discovered that the reason she "broke up" with him was because her grandfather had told her that white people should be with white people and black people should be with black people. Oof!

As parents, we could have taken this opportunity to embrace Münchausen's and infuse our son with a victim mentality, to turn him against white people by painting them with a broad brush and making it out to seem like this grandfather's horrendous attitude was the norm instead of the exception. We could have encouraged him to make that unfair experience central to his identity and taught him to harbor resentment—not only against this particular girl and her family, but against white people or society as a whole. Instead, we explained that this individual is ignorant and that there are, indeed, people in this world (of all skin colors) who foolishly believe that skin color matters. We made it clear that such a view is not only wrong, but it is extremely toxic and that, while some people will choose to live their lives in such a miserable fashion, we refuse to participate in their misery.

People often have a difficult time understanding my family's perspective on race. They can't fathom how we are able to disconnect ourselves from the contrived importance of racial identity and raise our children outside of it. We are currently in the process of adopting a child, and the application form included a portion asking us to list the race of each member of our household. We initially wrote "N/A" on that, but our adoption agency wanted us to put *something*. But why must we answer that? Why must we adhere to a given racial identity? Why must we put a racial identity on our children? What is the purpose?

Consider for a moment the arbitrary nature of racial classification. I am considered to be part of the black race. But no one else in the world has my exact ancestry and the phenotypical expression of it. No one. My genetic makeup is unique to me. My physical features are unique to me. Even my two brothers are distinct from me, and we have many obvious differences. So, if we are to define race by ancestral heritage and physical traits, then I can be considered a race in and of myself. And if we dampen the resolution a bit further, allowing for more variability in ancestry and physicality, then we can expand the scope to include my children, who share many similarities with both me and my wife. Therefore, my wife, our kids, and I could feasibly be considered a race.

In fact, this sort of familial perspective used to be the meaning of the word "race." It referred strictly to family lines, not skin colors.

Merriam-Webster lists this definition for race: "The descendants of a common ancestor. A group sharing a common lineage."[6] In *A Tale of Two Cities* by Charles Dickens, Dr. Alexandre Manette reveals how he discovered that the Marquis St. Evrémonde and his brother had raped and murdered a young woman, her husband, and her brother. The Marquis and his brother had Dr. Manette locked away in the Bastille for eighteen years after he tried to expose what they had done. While imprisoned, Dr. Manette wrote a letter denouncing the Evrémonde family, stating that they "and their descendants, to the last of their race" will pay the price.[7] He was not talking about physical features or ethnicity. He was talking about the specific family. The Evrémondes were a race.

So by this definition, my kids should be considered a part of the "Johnson" race. Why not? If common ancestry is to be the metric, why *shouldn't* racial classification be restricted to families? But even then, we must ask how far back should we go? Which common ancestor do we choose? Should we base our choice on the line from our maternal or paternal grandparents? Everyone has eight great-grandparents and sixteen great-great-grandparents, and this number continues to expand exponentially as you travel backward through the family tree. How far should we travel and which of these innumerable lines do we follow? What level of commonality qualifies? Is only one common ancestor sufficient? How common do our ancestries have to be to consider ourselves members of the same race? And wouldn't such a metric actually disqualify "black" from being considered a race, since the African ancestors of so-called "black people" all came from various African countries and cultures without any real shared ancestry? Or is simply having ancestors from the continent of Africa enough? If so, should South Africans like Elon Musk and Charlize Theron be included? Aren't they African-American? If we don't rely on family lines, common ancestry, or geography, should we rely on skin tone? What about lower-caste Indian people, who often have darker skin? Are they black? What about those of African ancestry who have pale skin? The criteria of "race" is wholly arbitrary.

It is worth noting that CRT, bizarrely contradicting itself, does claim that race is, indeed, a social construct rather than a biological reality. But it does this while simultaneously treating race as objective, biological, and permanent (while also clinging to relativism and claiming objectivity does not exist) and assigning meaning and moral value to it. If its advocates truly believe that race is a contrived social construct and the goal is truly to dismantle racism, then one would think such an endeavor would include an objective to dismantle race itself. There should be a movement to eliminate racial collectivism and to embrace individualism. Yet, instead, we see the opposite behavior.

The problem should be clear. The racial categorizations CRT advocates use are and have always been nonsensical and unnecessarily divisive, as well as the direct source of racial hostility. Often, proponents rebut this by saying "black" refers to culture, not race. This is false, but it helps highlight the problem we are addressing here. Certainly, there are subcultures to which some so-called black people subscribe and in which they participate. But if categorization were truly only about culture, then there would be no need to cling to race at all.

However, when I suggest this, I am met with anger and called names. Surely, if it were only about culture and not race, then suggesting that we let go of race would not be met with such hostility. If race were not important, "white" people who embrace such cultures could be called "black"—not unlike people who embrace the emo or gaming cultures. There is no racial gatekeeping for these subcultures. If white people can be emo or gamers by embracing those subcultures, why can't they be called black by embracing so-called "black culture"? The response would be that white people do not have the correct ancestry.

This line of argument gives the game away. It *is* about race, not culture. These aren't cultures that came from different countries, like the Italian or Irish cultures (neither of which depend on skin color). The distinction can only be racial. So again, we end up with a categorization issue. Who can be considered black? What *is* the correct ancestry? Must you have slaves in your family tree? If so, how many? What if you also descend from slave owners? What if you descend from *black* slave owners? How pure does your blood have to be? Shall we return to the one-drop rule, which classified people as "Negro" if they had a single African ancestor? If so, wouldn't all of us be considered "black"?

The differing amounts of melanin in one's skin—which determines its darkness or lightness—is nothing more than a genetic adaptation based on the geographical location of a particular group of people. If we go back far enough in human history, we'll see that we all come from common ancestors who had darker skin (including "white" people). Mankind's origins, from the time of Adam and Eve, are rooted in Africa and the Middle East. When some of these humans later migrated to chillier climates with less sunlight (and thus, less exposure to ultraviolet light, paler skin became more advantageous for absorbing the UV light that was available—a key function in the synthesis of Vitamin D). Those paler people did not magically change into a different kind of human being. They did not suddenly become a different "race." They were still the same humans. They merely adapted to their environment.

Genetically, every human being on Earth is around 99.5 percent identical. Additionally, there is often more genetic variability between two people of the same supposed race than between two people of different races.[8] Race, as a biological concept, simply does not exist.

In considering these issues, I am often reminded of J. K. Rowling's *Harry Potter* novels and her handling of purebloods vs. mudbloods (an offensive term for wizards and witches who descended from both magical and non-magical people). Those characters who emphasized "pureblood" status are clearly the villains of the story and their views are repugnant to the reader. I have often wondered how we can so keenly recognize the evil in these ways of thinking when highlighted in popular culture, but not in our everyday lives. We read books or watch films that include these topics, and it is clear to us that drawing such arbitrary dividing lines between ourselves based on immutable characteristics that we can't control is the mark of a villain, not a hero. So why do we continue to do it?

My children are not some group collective. Their identity does not come from a racial categorization or immutable characteristics. Their identity comes from Christ. They each have their own individual personalities and interests wholly divorced from any of their physical traits. They are unique human beings, and that is what we emphasize in our household. While there will always be others in the world who care deeply about things like skin color and racial identity, our family does not.

One would think such views would be uncontroversial, but those who adhere to Critical Race Theory see me and my wife as ignorant, oppressive parents. They see us as people who enable white supremacy and systems of oppression, raising self-hating children who will be ill-equipped to protect themselves and others against the horrors of racial discrimination. I have often been accused of being a race traitor who hates his own people, of ignoring the problems of racism for his own personal gain, and therefore acting as a sort of accomplice to the perpetuation of these supposedly racist systems. In other words, if I don't embrace victimhood and the presuppositions of CRT and instill this sense of racialized illness in my children or teach them that the world is out to get them, that their failures and mistakes are due to racism, and that the white supremacist boogeyman lies in wait around every corner, then I have failed as a father. If I don't fight for educational standards and expectations to be lowered for my children so they can compete with white students, if I don't teach them to view every negative interaction as a racist microaggression, if I don't impress upon them the importance of demanding penance and recompense from others for historical injustices that they did not even experience and the accused did not even participate in, then I have failed as a father. If I refuse to automatically attribute disparities in outcomes to racial discrimination and refuse to teach my kids to see everyone and everything through the lens of race, I have failed as a father.

Hostile Attribution Bias

What do you think the impact would be if I taught my children to view the world the way CRT activists do? How would that affect their growth and development? How would it affect their relationships with their family and friends? How would that impact their mental health?

Imagine, for a moment, a non-racial scenario in which a child is led to believe that others are perpetually hostile toward him, for whatever reason. If a child begins to believe that everything another person says or does is secretly meant to hurt him, imagine what that would do to that child's psyche. There is actually a psychological term for this. It's called the Hostile Attribution Bias, and it describes that exact scenario: the persistent belief that others are secretly engaging in hostile behavior toward you even though the behavior is not overtly hostile. If someone glances at you, you will interpret it as a hostile glance. If someone laughs near you, you assume they are laughing at you. If you hear someone whispering, you assume they are whispering unflattering things about you. It is a wholly dysfunctional existence. Extensive research has supported the fact that such disordered thought processes are associated with higher levels of physical and relational aggression in children as well as poor outcomes for adults, including shorter life spans and significant relationship problems.[9] What, then, might be the impact when adding in the emotional baggage of race and racism to this dysfunctional psychology?

Why should we continue to do this to ourselves? Why should we continue to do this to our children? Why should we encourage adults to pass on their own brokenness, prejudices, anger, resentment, vengefulness, guilt, paranoia, and victimhood, etc. to children? Far too often, innocent children are handed this cup of racial poison by their parents, drink from it, and then pass that cup on to others so that they, too, can drink. It is a generational curse. It is the Fall of Man. It is Eve sharing the apple with Adam after having eaten from it herself, believing the manipulative tales whispered by the conniving serpent, convinced that embracing this curse will somehow bring about wisdom and enlightenment. "Ye shall not surely die." It is, and always has been, a lie.

It is ironic that those who adhere to Critical Race Theory demand that we engage in the same dysfunctional thought processes surrounding race that led to the past injustices they claim to be rectifying. How can you fight racism with racism? How can you cure a disease by inducing more disease?

I don't believe our country can thrive if we don't see each other as fellow countrymen and raise our children to do the same. If we don't acknowledge some sort of shared values, shared national identity, and a shared sense of brotherhood, we will tear our nation apart with our own hands. Further, when the arbitrary classification of race is treated as the defining characteristic of who a person is in America, it can have no other outcome than the disastrous outcomes it has had in the past. It can only end in pain and suffering. It seems to me a mistake to believe that the ideology underlying Jim Crow is somehow different from the ideology underlying Critical Race Theory, Black Lives Matter, antiracism, or any other race-obsessed movement. It has always been an ideology that inherently drives a wedge between ourselves and our neighbors on the basis of skin color and pits us against one another. We are continually separated into "us" and "them." When that dichotomy is rooted in grievance, as it often is, and passed down to subsequent generations, the situation is ripe for hostility. It breeds generational pathology. We are seeing that tragedy play out in our country at the present moment. I cannot speak for everyone, but I personally do not want to live in a world where children are held responsible for the sins of their ancestors or heralded as victims who inherit the grievances of those who came before them simply because they share a similar skin color. It is an evil, dysfunctional existence.

There is, indeed, a deep sickness permeating our society and infiltrating our institutions, but it isn't white supremacy. It is progressivism. It is obsession with racial identity. It is ideologies like Critical Race Theory. We must inoculate ourselves against this virus and find a way to exist as a single nation without seeing ourselves constantly reduced to our immutable characteristics and distributed into various identity groups—only to have those groups go to war with each other. We must abolish these toxic ideas of collective guilt and collective victimhood and refuse to instill them in our children. We must recognize that racial divisions are a false illusion that must be erased. We must see that we are one people in this country; there is no black history, brown history, or white history, only American history. We must refuse to teach our children that they are sick or induce symptoms of illness in them, shaping their identities around it. We must teach them to be victors, not victims. We must be one nation, under God, indivisible. We must transcend race.

CHAPTER 3

That's Not CRT!

You wish to be called righteous rather than act right . . .
I say, wrong must not win by technicalities.

—Aeschylus

Chances are, if you have ever voiced concerns about race-centric curricula in public schools or elsewhere, you have almost certainly been told that Critical Race Theory is not being taught or have been met with an exclamation of "That's not CRT!" These are the habitual responses to any criticism of how progressive race activists are handling the issues of race and racism in our society. What needs to be understood is that this is nothing more than semantic obfuscation. It is a game of language manipulation meant to intentionally obscure the issue at hand while making a technical argument to deflect from the concerns being voiced. It is akin to, when I tell my son not to punch his sister, he kicks her instead and then says, "Well, technically, I didn't punch her!"

As we discussed in Chapter 1, there are both academic and activist elements to Critical Race Theory; its founders and adherents have both openly acknowledged this. CRT was never meant to be confined to textbooks and classroom theory. It was meant to be implemented into the structure of society, and utilized as a mechanism for radical social transformation. This activist element to CRT encourages those trained in its edicts to actively implement them wherever they are in the world. It is quite literally a tool for revolution.

Despite educators' protestations that CRT is not being taught to children, this call for activism includes education. Universities are open about training future educators in the principles of CRT, and the teachers who have internalized this training are absolutely implementing it into their classrooms and lesson plans. But they are correct that, technically, they aren't *teaching* it.

Do you see the sleight of hand? They can claim that they aren't teaching CRT in schools because what they're actually doing is implementing their training. It is application. They are treating CRT's dogmatic assertions as incontrovertible truth and filtering their lesson plans through it. It is not Critical Race Theory so much as it is Critical Race *Praxis*. Clearly, elementary students are not reading and analyzing Derrick Bell's essays or taking home CRT textbooks to read for homework, but teachers are still having their white students deconstruct their whiteness, still pushing ideology surrounding the supposed problems of systemic racism, and still training their students to see the world as a Marxist dichotomy of racial victims and oppressors. This is the distinction. It is not being taught so much as it is being applied.

Adherents to race-based education will insist that what is being used in classrooms or corporate training seminars is somehow different from Critical Race Theory. They will attach a different name to it and pretend the two are separate. They will attempt to draw a line between CRT and antiracism or between CRT and equity initiatives. They will proclaim that parents, or anyone who accuses them of teaching CRT, don't actually understand what CRT is, and therefore, their opinions should be dismissed. Again, this is just a way to muddy the waters. It is a tactic meant to cause confusion and uncertainty. It attempts to elevate CRT to some sort of esoteric concept that can only be understood by someone with a doctorate degree and cannot possibly be grasped by ignorant, bigoted parents.

At the same time, however, many of these activists will openly admit to implementing CRT into classrooms during seminars and training sessions when they believe they are among like-minded people. But when the audience is hostile, they will deny it. In July 2022, the African American Policy Forum held a Zoom event called "CRT Summer School" in which panelists discussed topics such as "Everyday CRT in K-12," "How to Teach about Race," "Organizing and Teaching against White Narratives in Social Studies Textbooks," and "CRT Education and Legislative Action." They decried anti-CRT arguments as right-wing disinformation campaigns while openly claiming to teach educators how to take "proactive, collective action to expand antiracist teaching and learning . . . building our capacity to engage in collaborative, sustaining work that puts our principles into practice."[1] To paraphrase, it is egregious, right-wing disinformation to claim that CRT is being taught in public schools, but also, let us show you how you can further teach CRT in public schools.

The dishonesty is obvious. Clearly, CRT is in public schools. But in the grand scheme of things, the arguments about what is and what isn't CRT are largely irrelevant regardless of their merit (or lack thereof). It doesn't really matter what label we attach to what's going on in these classrooms—the virus is still a virus, and the poison is still poison—even if you paint the container in bright, beautiful colors and tell us it's medicine.

Consider these examples:

In New York City, the principal of East Side High School sent a survey to parents instructing them to rate their whiteness on a scale ranging from "white supremacist" to "white abolitionist." The scale was developed by Barnor Hesse, a professor of African American Studies at Northwestern University, and states that

> There is a regime of whiteness and there are action-oriented white identities. People who identify with whiteness are one of these. It's about time we build an ethnography of whiteness, since white people have been the ones writing about and governing others.[2]

The California Department of Education has implemented something it calls the "California Mathematics Framework," which aims to eliminate gifted programs and advanced classes due to their allegedly "racially biased" nature. The creators also seek to center curricula (even in hard sciences like mathematics) around racial equity and "sociopolitical consciousness."[3]

In Oregon, Portland City Schools implemented a "Racial Educational Equity Policy" which bemoans the achievement gaps between white and non-white students, and vows to "address and overcome this inequity and institutional racism."[4]

In Massachusetts, Boston Public Schools suspended the entrance exam for advanced classes in the name of racial equity due to the fact that low numbers of black and brown students were passing it. Superintendent Brenda Cassellius said, "There's a lot of work we have to do in the district to be antiracist and have policies where all of our students have a fair shot at an equitable and excellent education."[5]

The Arizona Department of Education created an "equity toolkit" for babies, which suggests that white babies begin showing signs of racism by three months of age, and that white children have solidified their white supremacy by age five. Therefore, the department says, white parents must take an active role in deconditioning them and implementing antiracist parenting tactics.[6]

The International Society for Technology in Education offers extensive teaching resources for educators on how to "nurture antiracism in children."[7]

Arizona State University has implemented something called the "Children's Equity Project" which "focuses on closing opportunity gaps and dismantling systemic racism in learning settings."[8]

In my own state of Ohio, Columbus City Schools proclaims it has now "taken a strong stance and has begun steps to end the systemic racism that has existed for 175 years within the Columbus City Schools education system and is dedicated to further reforms."[9]

Also in Ohio, Mentor Public Schools used training materials for teachers that included shaping education through a "social and racial justice lens," urging teachers to become "co-conspirators" (i.e., embracing antiracist ideology and activism) and claiming that traditional education curricula is "rooted in whiteness."[10]

These are but a few examples among thousands demonstrating how race-obsessed ideology has infiltrated the public school systems, childhood education initiatives, and even parenting programs all over the country. One only needs to search for the name of a school—particularly one in a left-leaning area of the country—along with the term "antiracism," and the results will be apparent. School systems often vehemently deny teaching Critical Race Theory, yet they proudly tout the race-centric policies born from its presuppositions: that racism is ubiquitous and that racial disparities are evidence of systemic racism. They shroud their racist policy in feel-good emotional language like "equity" and "diversity," but no matter what you call it, the results are the same: racial discrimination.

The Bigotry of Low Expectations

These race activists have no problem admitting that their policies are based on antiracism and racial equity (meaning the pursuit of equal outcomes, not opportunities) and that they specifically target what they claim to be institutional/systemic racism. This comes directly out of the Critical Race Theory ideological framework. Why deny it? Additionally, it is worth noting that equal outcomes cannot possibly be achieved unless the higher achievers are brought down to the level of the lower achievers. This is why schools are eliminating advanced classes and gifted programs, and why they are doing away with standardized testing or loosening grammar requirements to be more racially inclusive. In order to create an equitable environment, educators must discriminate based on race.

This brings us to another glaring problem with race-based educational policy: its deleterious impact on non-white students. When you lower educational standards for them, you are engaged in a particularly pernicious form of racism yourself. As was discussed previously, Critical Race Theory seems to promote the belief that one can fight perceived racism by engaging in racism. Most apparent is the racism targeted at white people, but what is even more insidious is the racism aimed at non-white people—the people these policies are purporting to help. It is, as former President George W. Bush termed it, "the soft bigotry of low expectations." I would argue that there is nothing soft about it. It is outright bigotry. It is the belief that non-white students, because they are non-white, require special accommodations and allowances in order to compete with white students; meanwhile, the white students either get no such accommodations or are actively handicapped in some fashion. This is called "fairness." This is called "equity." This is called "justice." Those who engage in this bigotry claim that it is unfair to expect black students to speak or write with proper English grammar, to arrive on time, to expect them to stay in their seats or be quiet and well-behaved during class, or to be able to comprehend mathematical concepts, etc. For example, Marcus Moore, a trainer with Courageous Conversation, argued that white culture is obsessed with "the King's English rules," "objective, rational, linear thinking," "quantitative emphasis," and "rigid time schedules." He said that obsession with "clock time" and punishing students for being late is "but one example of how whiteness undercuts Black kids."[11] According to Moore, intentional measures must be set in place to ensure that black students are not made to "bend to whiteness." Additionally, because white students happen to comprise the majority of advanced and "gifted-and-talented" classes at a given school, administrators claim that the advanced classes themselves are racist and cater to white students who don't actually deserve their accomplishments, and therefore, the classes must be abolished.[12] This is racism, and no matter what label they attach to it, it is absolutely Critical Race Theory.

Public schools have been having similar problems with Queer and Gender Theory, which are beyond the scope of this book. Ultimately, it all points to a question I have been asking for a few years now: Can public schools be salvaged? I do not pretend that every school is infected by this disease, but it is so widespread and so embedded that the entire structure appears to be corrupted beyond redemption. It seems to have been a mistake to put the government in charge of our children's education and to create a scenario where they must attend school where they live—meaning that the normal market forces that exist in a competitive market are not present. Some states have worked to change this, giving parents choice and allowing education dollars to follow the student. Elsewhere, where this is not the case, teachers, teachers' unions, and politicians are not beholden to parents as a business would be to its customers. They pay no price and have no incentive to change. Meanwhile, they demand ever-increasing amounts of taxpayer dollars for ever-decreasing academic results.

It should be no surprise that parents are upset. What loving parent would want teachers and administrators to make decisions about their children based on their race? What parent would want teachers to have lower expectations for their children than they do for other students based on their skin color? It is the same problem dealt with during the post-Civil War era and the civil rights movement. It is the same kind of broken, racist thinking that groups students into racial collectives and makes judgments about them based on those collectives. It is the same racism.

I find it interesting that people so vehemently deny that Critical Race Theory is being implemented in public school classrooms when it is patently obvious that it is. They also clearly believe in its claims and underlying assumptions. So why distance themselves from it? If they believe in it so deeply, why not teach it in classrooms? Wouldn't it be a good thing to teach it to children? These questions are never answered because the purpose is deflection. They know what they are doing. They know it isn't popular. They know that people would resist if they knew what was actually happening. So, they play a game of technicalities in order to obscure the truth.

Of course, CRT was never really even about the name itself, anyway. It was about the behavior. So if you find yourself in an argument about whether CRT is taught in schools, it might be prudent to remember that your opponent is attempting to obfuscate the issue, and that ultimately, it makes no real difference what it's called. The name is not important. Teaching a victim/oppressor worldview, infusing Marxist ideology, and treating students differently on the basis of their race should be wholly rejected whether it's called Critical Race Theory; Diversity, Equity, and Inclusion; or anything else.

CHAPTER 4

The Motte and the Bailey

The Party told you to reject the evidence of your eyes and ears. It was their final, most essential command.

—George Orwell

Have you ever heard someone push some extreme position in an argument and then, when you challenge them on it, they retreat to some milder, less controversial position? Imagine a child making an argument for eating candy for breakfast. When the parents refuse and dismantle the logic of this argument, the child retreats to a simple and manipulative, "I just think parents should want their kids to be happy."

This is the motte-and-bailey tactic. It is a term coined by Nicholas Shackel, a professor of philosophy at Oxford University. It references the structure of a motte-and-bailey castle which has a large, poorly protected courtyard (the bailey) and an elevated, heavily fortified structure (the motte) to which the people can retreat when the bailey is under attack. In likewise fashion, when people employ the motte-and-bailey tactic, they put forth a controversial argument that is difficult to defend, then retreat to the much less controversial motte when the bailey is attacked.

In the previous example, no one would ever disagree with the argument, "Parents should want their kids to be happy." Of course parents want their kids to be happy. However, that doesn't make the argument for eating candy for breakfast valid. The conflation of the two arguments is the ultimate goal. You must accept that eating candy for breakfast is a valid argument because you accept the argument that parents should want their children to be happy. By retreating to the motte, the arguer hopes to make the bailey more difficult to attack.

Once you recognize this tactic, you will begin to see it everywhere. Critical Race Theory adherents use it heavily, but you see it all throughout progressivism and politics in general. You will see it when radical gender activists insist that transgender people should be treated like humans, as if anyone disagrees with that. You will see it in abortion debates when pro-choice advocates declare that women should have the right to bodily autonomy. You will see it in the halls of Congress and in the media when radical election policies are presented as being "for the people." What generally coincides with these fallacies is a strawman argument: if you reject the bailey, your opponents pretend that you rejected the motte. If you reject the idea of infinite gender pronouns or men playing women's sports, they will pretend you are saying transgender people should be mistreated and abused. If you reject the arguments behind abortion and argue for the basic right to life, they will pretend you are against the right to bodily autonomy and want to regulate women's bodies. If you reject the outrageous policies of the Democrat Party and voice concerns about voter fraud and federalizing elections, they will pretend you support disenfranchising minorities.

Likely, you can already think of numerous other examples of this tactic being applied in political discussions. We will discuss a few as it pertains to Critical Race Theory in this chapter, but ultimately, the entire approach of CRT is one giant motte-and-bailey argument.

Every scenario is presented as if it is something else, and every challenge is deflected by retreating to a less controversial position—usually with some sort of appeal to emotion. Some examples of these mottes include claims such as, "We just want to teach true history," "We just want equality," "We just want to combat racism," "We just want to teach children to be inclusive," or even "CRT is a graduate-level course," as we discussed in the last chapter.

Few people will argue against teaching accurate history, seeking equality, or fighting racism. But these terms do not mean what leftists purport them to mean. When they say they want to teach "true history," they mean teaching subjective interpretations of history that center everything around slavery while establishing white racism against black and brown people as the focal point. When they say they want equality, they actually mean pursuing equity and policies that discriminate against white people in favor of non-white people. When they say they want to combat racism, they mean they want to create social justice warriors who will internalize the presuppositions of Critical Race Theory and see themselves and others primarily through the lens of race and conceptualize all relationships through racial power dynamics. When they say they want children to be inclusive, they mean they want children to bow down to progressivism and embrace radical race and gender ideology. The less controversial claims are used to shield the delivery of radical ideas.

The Kafka Trap

Think of slogans like "Black Lives Matter" or "antiracism." The creators incorporate the motte into the very names. Who will disagree with the idea that black lives matter? Who is not against racism? It is a clever way to conceal true motives and deflect criticism. After the George Floyd incident, the media essentially forbade people from even questioning the motives of the Black Lives Matter movement; anyone who did was accused of racism or supporting racists. If you opposed the BLM riots and the horrific violence that occurred all over the country in the summer of 2020, you were accused of being a person who believes black lives do not matter. If you questioned the shady practices of the BLM organization and rejected its openly Marxist views, it could only be because you are a white supremacist.

The same pattern follows the antiracism movement. Any opposition to its goals and ideology is determined to be due to racism. If you are not an antiracist, you are clearly pro-racism. Proponents claim that since racism is supposedly ubiquitous in the system, any denial of its existence and subsequent opposition to eliminating it is direct evidence of racism and driven by a desire to perpetuate it. This is known as a Kafka Trap—an assertion of guilt that can never be disproven, no matter what you do. One must either confess to the crime they are accused of, which makes them guilty, or they declare their innocence, which also makes them guilty. Since guilty people nearly always declare that they are innocent, doing so automatically makes you guilty. Ibram X. Kendi has used this tactic on a regular basis while promoting his antiracism agenda, proclaiming nonsense like, "Denial is the heartbeat of racism," which suggests that racist people deny that they are racist, so therefore, denial is actually evidence of racist guilt.

The Kafka Trap—a term that comes from Franz Kafka's 1925 novel *The Trial*—goes hand in hand with the motte-and-bailey and the dishonest tactics that surround ideologies like Critical Race Theory. It is called a "trap" for a reason. It is not unlike loaded questions that cannot be answered without also accepting the given premise and admitting guilt. The classic example is, "When did you stop beating your wife?" To answer the question, you must accept the premise that you had been beating your wife in the first place. The only way out of such a trap is to reject the premise. Reject the premise that you beat your wife. Reject the premise that racism is endemic. Call out the tactics and expose them for what they are.

I once had a debate with a CRT advocate who insisted that it was extremely dangerous to be a black person in America given the state of white supremacy and racist policing. I pointed her to statistics that demonstrated that black people are only in significant danger of being killed by other black people, and that police are actually more likely to kill white suspects (we will discuss this later). Her response was that the statistics themselves were racist and should therefore be discarded. Never mind that she tried to use statistics initially to make her argument! In her mind, her statistics were accurate and acceptable, but my statistics were racist, since they rebutted her narrative.

The conversation was predictably less than fruitful. The woman eventually retreated to her motte and declared that she was just trying to make the world better for black people and didn't understand why I would be against that. When I rejected this manipulative tactic, she accused me of knowingly benefitting from white privilege, hating black people, being a mouthpiece for white supremacy, and intentionally ignoring the "obvious" systemic racism in this country. There was nothing I could say or any evidence I could provide to convince her otherwise. There was no reasoning with her. My denial was evidence of my guilt. Her ideas on systemic racism were so entrenched, and the ideological grip of CRT was so tight, that anything that might disprove them was seen as further evidence of systemic racism and my internalized white supremacy.

Two Movies, One Screen

It is clear that people on either side of these issues are often operating in completely separate realities. I believe it was Scott Adams, the creator of the cartoon *Dilbert*, who said that our modern era of politics is like two people watching two movies on the same screen. In reality, it is only a single movie, but the people watching it are so polarized that they are seeing entirely different (and often even completely opposite) things.

This is precisely what happens when there is any perceived racial incident. The two sides approach the issue from completely different universes. How do we resolve that problem? It is even more difficult to bridge the gap when there isn't even a common language and the meanings of words are changed on the fly.

As we discussed in Chapter 1, Critical Race Theory is notorious for manipulating language. The transformation of definitions is integral to the motte-and-bailey tactic and adds another layer of obfuscation. When a seemingly innocuous concept is presented, such as "justice" or "accountability," it is done with the obvious purpose of making it difficult to refute. Once again, few people would reject the concept of justice or have any real issue with people being held accountable for their actions. The problem, however, comes from what leftists actually mean by "justice" and "accountability." To those who embrace CRT, "justice" does not mean neutral principles of law, due process, or fairness. It actually means committing acts of retribution against people they deem to be responsible for historical inequity—and this extends well beyond the actual supposed perpetrators, like slaveholders, onto their descendants and even those who merely share the same skin color. For example, Critical Race Theory would look at a statistical wealth disparity between racial groups (*these* statistics are apparently not racist and can be trusted), determine that the disparity is due to systemic racial discrimination, and aim to redistribute wealth from twenty-first-century white families to black families.

That is not even remotely what most people are thinking of when they hear the word "justice." But that's what CRT advocates mean.

The word "accountability" operates the same way. CRT advocates believe accountability should be multigenerational and race-based. That means that even if you are not in any way racist and have not done anything discriminatory in your life, if you are white, you are still supposedly benefitting from a racist system. As such, you have a responsibility to acknowledge and correct that injustice. If you do not, you must be held accountable for perpetuating systems of oppression. Even the progressive definition of the word "racism" itself does not mean what most people think it means. It's all manipulation.

Another word that gets wholly distorted is "rights." When CRT advocates talk about rights, they really only mean positive rights, not negative rights. Negative rights involve freedom *from* things, like coercion or someone forcing their will on you. It means that others cannot compel you to do anything. By contrast, positive rights involve being provided with something, such as housing, health care, food, education, a job with a certain level of wages, etc.

These two ideas are in direct conflict. They cannot possibly coexist. For example, if a person believes that housing is a right, they must also believe that someone should be forced to provide housing. That is the only way it could possibly be a right. If someone believes they have a right to health care, they must also believe that someone else should be forced to provide it for them free of charge. It is impossible to demand that you have a right to be given food without also forcing someone else to grow it for you. The very existence of a positive right cancels the idea of negative rights because positive rights inherently require coercion. Clearly, things like food and housing are important and we want people to have them, but to claim that they are "rights" would mean that people should have them even at the expense of another person's rights. Critical Race Theory champions this idea of positive rights while denigrating negative rights. To its proponents, negative rights perpetuate systems of oppression.

(Honestly, at this point, it may be simpler to ask these people what *doesn't* perpetuate systems of oppression.)

Discussion between the two sides is nearly impossible because we cannot agree on even basic facts about reality. We can't agree on language and definitions. So how can there be communication?

It isn't clear to me that communication is even a goal of CRT beyond what is required to compel people to accept its ideas. Much of the movement involves browbeating people into fealty, maligning opponents as racists, and declaring that human rights are not up for debate (there's that word "rights" again). It is infused into public school curricula, corporate training seminars, and government policies as if it is objective truth and established fact. Those who oppose it are treated as if they are opposing gravity itself. In that sense, the motte-and-bailey tactic quells discussion and debate. The subtext is "Just shut up and go along with it." And unfortunately, many people do.

Tu Quoque and Christians

One other common tactic that is utilized along with the motte-and-bailey and Kafka Trap is the Tu Quoque Fallacy, or the Appeal to Hypocrisy. This is an attempt to dismiss an argument by claiming that the person making it has engaged in behavior inconsistent with its conclusions. It is fallacious reasoning because instead of addressing the argument's merit, the opponent attacks the person. There are many examples of this tactic being employed in our culture at the moment, but what interests me most is how it relates to Christians who oppose Critical Race Theory.

I have found that progressives who are not Christians love to tell Christians what the Bible says. They love to misquote Biblical verses, proclaim that Jesus was a radical socialist, and try to teach everyone their twisted version of theology. They don't actually believe in any of it, but that isn't the point; the point is to use Christian values and beliefs against those who do believe in order to bend them to the will of progressivism. They will proclaim that Christians are supposed to love their neighbors. They will say that Jesus was an advocate for justice. They will say that Christianity demands that we fight for equity. And they will claim that the Bible supports their position—regardless of what their position is and regardless of what the Bible actually says.

Of course, Christianity *does* require that we love our neighbors and value justice. But how that manifests is wholly dependent on how you define "love" and "justice." It is clear that we are not using even remotely the same definitions of those words. The point here is to attempt to hide the bailey by retreating to the motte and claiming that the opponents are hypocrites in order to invalidate them.

For instance, if you questioned the facts about actor Jussie Smollett claiming he was attacked by a couple of white supremacists in Chicago yelling, "This is MAGA country!" while pouring bleach on him and hanging a noose around his neck, CRT advocates angrily asked, "How can you support hate crimes as a Christian if Christianity demands that you love your neighbor and value justice?" If you push back on Kendi's book *How to Be an Antiracist* being a part of your child's school curriculum, they will wonder aloud, "Why would Christians support racism when their Bible teaches against it?" If you reject government equity policies that discriminate against white people in favor of non-white people on the basis of race, they will say, "Christians are supposed to help those in need." Once again, it is the "When did you stop beating your wife?" question. It is loaded with an inaccurate premise shielded by deceptive phrasing that is then used as a cudgel. Over and over again, they use this tactic. Is it truly loving to promote racial division? Is it truly justice to support lies and hate crime hoaxes? Is it truly biblical to infuse our children with an ideology of victimhood?

Unfortunately, many Christians have indeed found themselves sucked up into this erroneous reasoning. Phil Vischer, one of the creators of VeggieTales, spent an afternoon lecturing me on Twitter about antiracism, claiming that he was against racism while I was not. During a conference at Atlanta's Passion City Church in 2020, Chick-fil-A Chairman Dan Cathy shined the shoes of Christian rap artist Lecrae in a supposed act of penance and racial reconciliation.[1] There was an event in Houston where a group of white Christians knelt in front of a group of black Christians and asked them for forgiveness for racism.[2] There were churches that held "Black Lives Matter" services and posted large photos of George Floyd and splashed the words "Black Lives Matter" on their marquees and all over their materials and websites. The Evangelical Lutheran Church in America (ELCA) has an entire page on its website dedicated to promoting BLM and advancing antiracism causes.[3] The Presbyterian Church dedicates an entire section of its website to antiracism.[4] Many so-called "black churches" have made Critical Race Theory central to their theology and now preach social justice during sermons. The rot runs deep.

I suspect that some of this comes from good intentions. I also suspect that much of it stems from a desire for conformity and acceptance. It's easy to stand up for what you know is right when everyone is on your side and patting you on the back. It's much harder to do so when no one is on your side and there's a target on your back instead. Many churches, pastors, and Christians in general want to be accepted by people who hate them. And not just Christians, either; it is a general problem for conservatives. Progressives have captured much of our culture and, therefore, to oppose progressivism is quite literally to be countercultural. A lot of people don't want to do that. It is uncomfortable and often difficult. You could lose friends and even family members for having the wrong beliefs. Some people have lost their jobs and careers for voicing the wrong opinions. In some cases, angry mobs might even show up on your doorstep. That is a real issue. But people, Christians in particular, need to choose which god they are going to serve.

What many people don't seem to recognize is that Critical Race Theory is a large part of what essentially operates like an extremist religion: Those who embrace it quite literally worship race. They have original sin (i.e., racism), no tolerance for apostasy, demands for self-sacrifice and repentance of sins, holy texts, high priests who pass down the holy dogma which no one is permitted to challenge, evangelists who proselytize and spread the gospel while pursuing converts, inquisitors who search for and punish heretics, they have taboo, and they have a creation story in the 1619 Project. This means it is impossible for Christians to embrace both Christianity and CRT any more than they can simultaneously embrace Christianity and Islam. One must inevitably give way to the other. I suspect this is what's happening with these Christian leaders and organizations. They have embraced a different religion.

There Are Four Lights

Of course, one need not be a Christian to recognize the toxic destructiveness of CRT ideology. It is genuinely surprising when people fail to see the manipulative tactics at work. Even if you can't put a technical name to what's going on, the dishonesty and manipulation should be readily apparent. When some corporation says it wants to "elevate black voices" but intentionally ignores or outright dismisses black conservative voices, you know you are dealing with manipulation, not truth. When there are tears and celebration over the "blackness" of a woman who is appointed to the U.S. Supreme Court while longtime justice Clarence Thomas gets nothing but hatred and vitriol, you know you are dealing with manipulation and not truth. When a mass shooting committed by a white man gets unceasing media coverage and endless think pieces devoted to it while every mass shooting committed by a black man or incident in which a black nationalist mows down a bunch of white people at a Christmas parade gets swept into the memory hole, you know you are dealing with manipulation and not truth.

I am often reminded of the episode of *Star Trek: The Next Generation* in which Gul Madred tortures Captain Picard to try to force him to admit that there are five lights in the room even though there are clearly only four.[5] This episode was based on George Orwell's famous novel *Nineteen Eighty-Four*, in which the villain, O'Brien, tells the main character, Winston, to say how many fingers he is holding up. When Winston correctly answers, "Four," O'Brien responds, "And if the Party says that it is not four, but five—then how many?" Winston again answers, "Four," and is subjected to intense pain as a result. The torture continues until he is no longer able to resist submitting to the lie.[6]

In both of these scenarios, the entire point is to have such significant power and control over another person that you can get them to accept something as true that they know to be false, and vice versa. If you can get someone to admit that there are five lights when there are four, that two plus two equals five, or that racism is endemic in our society when it isn't, you have complete control over him.

I must point out that, like Winston, there was even a moment when Picard actually saw five lights. The line between lie and truth became so blurred that he was able to see the falsehood as objective reality. Like the old adage attributed to Joseph Goebbels, if you repeat a lie often enough, people will begin to believe it. Even you, yourself, will come to believe it. Such is the nature of human psychology.

This is what Critical Race Theory is about. It is manipulation. It is a quest for power and control. It is a series of fallacies and linguistic tricks that are meant to confuse, bully, and manipulate people into not just embracing blatant lies, but actually believing them. It demands that you see five lights when there are only four, or else you will be "reeducated" until you comply. It pretends to be something innocuous, something compassionate, while purposefully concealing its true and nefarious intentions. It is one giant—and extremely dangerous—motte-and-bailey.

CHAPTER 5

Justice and Vengeance

*Beloved, do not avenge yourselves, but rather give place
to wrath; for it is written, "Vengeance is Mine, I will
repay," says the Lord.*

—Romans 12:19

A common refrain among those who espouse the toxic ideology of antiracism and those who believe (or pretend to believe) in the fantasies of Critical Race Theory is, "We demand racial justice!" They scream this with their jaws set and fists raised. It is, yet again, that tactic of language manipulation that has become typical of progressivism, that nefarious game of semantics and emotional blackmail.

When a Kenosha, Wisconsin, police officer shot twenty-nine-year-old Jacob Blake in August 2020, Black Lives Matter protesters initiated a series of riots in the city. They burned numerous vehicles and at least forty buildings and caused an estimated $50 million worth of damage to property overall. While this was all happening, on the night of August 25, a seventeen-year-old named Kyle Rittenhouse showed up with a rifle and first aid kit to help people who were injured and protect businesses. At some point during the night, three individuals attacked Rittenhouse and chased him through the streets. One of the assailants had a gun and another attempted to beat Rittenhouse with a skateboard. Rittenhouse shot all three men in self-defense, killing two. For that, Rittenhouse was charged with murder, and his trial became a national spectacle. The jury would eventually agree with the self-defense argument, and Rittenhouse was rightfully acquitted.

BLM activists, politicians, and media talking heads widely called for racial justice both before and after the verdict. But what did they mean by this? Rittenhouse was white. All three of the people he shot were white. What did race have to do with anything? The fact that people had somehow turned it into a racial issue gives tremendous insight into the goals of CRT and what its advocates really mean when they say "justice."

Those demanding this so-called "racial justice" proclaimed Rittenhouse's acquittal to be unjust. And a few months later, when Gregory McMichael and his son Travis were convicted of a federal hate crime in the murder of twenty-five-year-old Ahmaud Arbery in Georgia, the same people proclaimed the results of that trial to be just. The validity of the outcomes aside, it needs to be understood that these activists did not arrive at either of these conclusions by examining evidence, seeking out objective truth, or trusting in due process. They came to them by looking at skin color and both historical and hypothetical grievances. To them, justice was served in the McMichaels' trial, not because of what the evidence said, but because white men had killed a black man. That was the only detail that mattered. But it did not matter that Rittenhouse was chased and beaten. It did not matter that one of his assailants was also armed. The focus was entirely on their determination that had Rittenhouse been black, he surely would have been sentenced to life in prison for shooting his assailants—that is, if police didn't kill him before he had the chance. Therefore, they claimed, justice was not served in his case. The fact that a black man named Andrew Coffee was acquitted of murder on the same day as Rittenhouse was dismissed and widely unreported because it did not support the narrative race activists had presented.

This is what activists mean by "racial justice." It means that the true ideals of justice must be overridden in the name of progressive ideology. Remember, to those who adhere to Critical Race Theory, the entire system is infested with racism and white supremacy and therefore, this inherently corrupt system can only produce inherently corrupted outcomes. That means that even if the evidence says someone is innocent, as was the case for Kyle Rittenhouse, it matters very little because to the CRT advocate, the system has concealed his guilt. The lack of evidence of guilt is seen as nothing more than further evidence of an institution overrun by systemic racism. If denial is the heartbeat of racism, then clearly lack of evidence is the heartbeat of racial injustice. The court of public opinion had already declared Rittenhouse guilty in the erroneous belief that a black person would have been treated differently regardless of his innocence. "Racial justice" demands penance for the crime of whiteness and the hypothetical crime of what might have happened to that person if he or she were black. It is imposing progressive dogma onto the scales of Lady Justice. It is ripping off her blindfold and fitting her with a pair of race-tinged glasses through which to view the law. It demands that she make judgments based not on facts and evidence, but on skin color and the emotions surrounding it.

This is how those who cling to the concept of racial justice believe truth should be determined. They believe guilt should be decided based on race, and then they seek out ways to rationalize that conclusion. It nearly always starts with some presumption reached through emotional reasoning. This is why the Rittenhouse case was littered with statements like "He crossed state lines," "He's a white supremacist," and "He shouldn't even have had a gun." The people saying those things were searching for reasons to justify the decision they had already made based on emotion, ideology, tribalism, and racial bigotry, not logic or reason. They had little interest in seeking out the truth.

Justice Does Not Need a Qualifier

This extension of the ideology should be no surprise, as Critical Race Theory is very direct about its mistrust of traditional justice. In fact, it is direct about its mistrust of all our institutions and founding principles. As we've established throughout this book, to the race-obsessed, the only important variable that needs to be analyzed is skin color, and the only culpability lies with white supremacy. It doesn't matter if a black man is violently attacking Jewish people in New York or Asian-Americans in California—white supremacy is still somehow to blame. It doesn't matter if a black gang member is gunning down a black child in a drive-by shooting—white supremacy is still somehow to blame. It doesn't matter if a white teenager defends himself against three white people during a riot—white supremacy is still somehow to blame.

If, like race activists, we consider objectivity to be a tool of the oppressor, then we must instead rely on irrational emotional reasoning within a race-centric worldview—infusing race into the equation at every turn, placing white supremacy at the pinnacle of the villain hierarchy, and adjusting our concept of justice accordingly. This, of course, is not justice at all.

If justice has an agenda, then it is not justice. If justice does not rely on facts and objective truth but on feelings, ideology, and the demands of a mob, then it is not justice. We again see the irony in how today's concept of "racial justice" is the same one used in the past to oppress other racial groups. The people who passed and enforced laws like Jim Crow rejected the principles of impartiality and objectivity for the sake of their own bigoted ideology and emotional reasoning. That was clearly not justice either, and for the same reasons. This is what happens when you vacate the concepts of liberalism and attempt to manipulate justice to serve your own agenda. This is what happens when you feel the need to qualify justice with words like "racial," "social," "climate," etc. The qualifier wholly distorts the purpose of justice.

No wonder our country appears to be hurtling backward through time. We are repeating the same mistakes that were already made. We are seeing racial discrimination in college admissions, segregation on college campuses, and criminal justice influenced by skin color, hatred, animosity, resentment, and hostility—all driven by this misguided idea of justice, which is enveloped by a perception of racial grievance and a desire for revenge.

We are supposed to believe that white supremacy is an elusive boogeyman perpetually lurking in the shadows. Grievances are claimed and punishments administered based solely on the presumed existence and influence of this all-powerful specter. An actual perpetrator—or even an actual victim—is not necessary to claim such grievances; symbolism will do just fine. Racial justice crusaders don't see people like Kyle Rittenhouse as human beings. They see them as abstract representations of white supremacy and obstacles to progressive ideology.

Racial justice does not care about actual justice. Racial justice seeks revenge for historical wrong and to advance the ideological agenda.

To this day, there has not been a single shred of evidence uncovered that even remotely suggests that George Floyd's death had anything whatsoever to do with his race. However, racial justice demanded (and continues to demand) that it be viewed that way. It demanded not only that the police officer, Derek Chauvin, be figuratively hanged as a white supremacist, but that anyone who questioned the details of the case at all were also white supremacists who should lose their jobs and have their lives destroyed. If you failed to post a black square on Instagram, you were maligned as a racist—or at best, a white supremacy sympathizer. The same was true in the police shootings of black people like Breonna Taylor, Rayshard Brooks, and Jacob Blake. No evidence ever surfaced that race had anything to do with any of those cases, but such facts are irrelevant and unpersuasive to the ideologue. Any opposition to the racial narrative presented was viewed as the perpetuation of systems of bigotry and racial violence, regardless of what the facts actually said. Evidence does not matter. All we need to know is that the supposed perpetrator was white and the supposed victim was black. No further analysis is required.

The ultimate point is that there cannot actually be such a thing as racial justice. There can only be justice. Justice cannot be driven by emotions, agendas, or ideology and still remain justice. When you consider terms like "racial justice," "social justice," "climate justice," etc., you recognize that they are just that: ideologically driven tactics of a progressive agenda. In the world of progressivism, whether something is considered "just" depends on whether it aligns with progressive ideology. In the context of racial justice, that means that there is no such thing as justice when CRT advocates don't get what they want. Everything they want is "justice"; everything they don't want is "injustice."

But according to our Founding Fathers, concepts like justice, due process, and even liberty itself exist to protect the people we don't like or agree with. This is vital to understand. They are meant to protect people you might prefer not to protect. If the only people for whom you ever want justice, due process, or liberty are people you like and agree with, then it is clear that you don't actually believe in those things at all. Why would we need due process if decisions can simply be made based on how we feel about the person in question? Why even have a trial? Just take a poll on Twitter and let the people decide. Of course, mob justice and witch trials seem like a great idea—until you're the one being accused.

It seems many people who behave this way don't consider this fact. They refuse to believe they could ever be on the receiving end of the horrors they either unleash themselves or allow to be unleashed on others. In the *Gulag Archipelago*, Aleksandr Solzhenitsyn describes how people in the Soviet Union under Joseph Stalin believed wholly in their innocence and thought they surely could not be secretly arrested in the middle of the night and sent off to a prison camp where they would be kept indefinitely.[1] After all, they personally hadn't done anything wrong, and they thought that those being arrested en masse must have been guilty.

The people who believed that were naïve. And so are we if we think we can rule by mob mentality without ever seeing the mob come for us, too.

What happens if it becomes acceptable to intimidate judges and juries into handing down a desired verdict, as race activists attempted in the Rittenhouse trial? Is such behavior acceptable as long as you believe your cause is morally righteous? Wouldn't that also mean that such behavior is always justified, no matter who's doing it, because everyone ultimately believes their cause is righteous? What are the implications of a system in which the desired outcomes are already predetermined and "injustice" simply means that a certain group of people do not get their way? What happens when people you dislike and disagree with engage in this version of justice based on *their* feelings of moral righteousness? Suddenly, the game isn't so fun anymore.

This is not how justice operates. It is not how justice should ever operate. Justice is blind, impartial, and fair. It does not depend on race, gender, sexuality, or ideology. It has nothing to do with what you want or how you feel. Therefore, there is no such thing as "racial justice." Justice is justice. It does not need a qualifier. When people feel the need to add one, you can be certain that we aren't talking about justice anymore.

Racial Grievance Identities

Booker T. Washington once said,

> There is another class of colored people who make a business of keeping the troubles, the wrongs, and the hardships of the Negro race before the public. Having learned that they are able to make a living out of their troubles, they have grown into the settled habit of advertising their wrongs—partly because they want sympathy and partly because it pays. Some of these people do not want the Negro to lose his grievances, because they do not want to lose their jobs. . . . There is a certain class of race problem-solvers who do not want the patient to get well, because as long as the disease holds out, they have not only an easy means of making a living, but also an easy medium through which to make themselves prominent before the public.[2]

This quote highlights the core of the problem with racial justice and the people we see leading the charge. The likes of Ibram Kendi, Kimberlé Crenshaw, Richard Delgado, Nikole Hannah-Jones, Ta-Nehisi Coates, Robin DeAngelo, Joy Reid, Jemele Hill, Al Sharpton, Jesse Jackson, Shaun King, Lebron James, Alexandria Ocasio-Cortez, Cori Bush, etc.—these people all thrive on racial division. They depend on it. Their very identities rely on the perception of endemic racism and oppression.

If your identity is rooted in victimhood, then you have an incentive to perpetuate it indefinitely. Otherwise, you become St. George the Dragon Slayer in retirement. That isn't permissible, so you will always try to maintain that victimhood identity and continually seek both sympathy and retribution. That's what Jussie Smollett was doing when he staged his own attack at the hands of some alleged white supremacists (actually fellow actors that he paid) in Chicago. That's what NASCAR driver Bubba Wallace was doing in June 2020 when he claimed someone had left a noose in his garage in an act of racial intimidation even though it turned out to be nothing more than a garage door pull rope that had been there since at least October 2019. It's what Vice President Kamala Harris was doing when she claimed that mispronouncing her name was an act of racism.[3]

This behavior is positively reinforced in our society. If MSNBC host Joy Reid goes on television and claims that some person she disagrees with is a racist white supremacist who is trying to get black people killed, or NBA star Lebron James claims that black people can't go outside without fear of being killed by white people, there will be no real consequences for such outrageous statements. Instead, tidal waves of support will flood in for them, people will lament how horrible America is, and the narrative that we need to pursue racial justice will be continually reinforced.

Because the people who promote racial justice often possess identities rooted in racial grievance (or a "white savior complex" if they are white), their idea of racial justice can never truly be achieved. And they don't actually want to achieve it. Talk of reparations, closing the wealth gap, eliminating other areas of racial disparity, complaining about discrimination, microaggressions, hidden racism, and historical impacts, etc. are nothing more than cudgels used to bludgeon their opponents and advance their own positions of power. This is most clearly seen in how issues such as inner-city crime and education are handled. Consider the fact that, according to the FBI Uniform Crime Report, nearly ten thousand black people nationwide were victims of homicide in 2020,[4] and, given the trends of previous years, it is almost certain that the vast majority of them were murdered by other black people (approximately 88 percent based on 2019 numbers).[5] This statistic was largely ignored. I have kept a running list of children under the age of thirteen who are murdered in street violence every year, and that list reached at least seventy-one children who were murdered in 2020 (at least seventy-eight the previous year), but there was virtually no national media coverage of those murders and very little talk of justice.

But when Ahmaud Arbery was killed, the entire country slammed to a standstill, and we were told we needed to reckon with the history of racism in our country; that it is extremely dangerous for black people to live in America; and that we are in desperate need of racial justice. How is it that this one death was considered to be so much more worthy of a media spotlight than the other nearly ten thousand combined?

When actor Terry Crews told CNN host Don Lemon that Black Lives Matter did not seem to care about the black lives of those murdered in street violence, Lemon's response was that BLM was only focused on police brutality.[6] The black lives ended through street violence apparently did not matter to Don Lemon—only the black lives ended by police. Also, his claim—that BLM only focuses on police brutality—clearly isn't even true, given the intense focus on cases like Arbery's, Jussie Smollett's, and seventeen-year-old Floridian Trayvon Martin's, none of whom were killed by police. But even beyond that, it is nonsensical for an organization that claims to be dedicated to convincing the world that black lives matter to limit its purview only to the black lives that comprise a miniscule percentage of overall homicides. Such behavior exposes the movement's dishonesty and underlying agenda. It is clear that race activists are only concerned with perpetuating the facade of racial oppression; therefore, only cases that provide support for a racial-grievance identity will be elevated. Cases that cannot be exploited and used to reinforce that identity will be blatantly and unapologetically ignored.

Enemy of the People

Lemon's exchange with Crews exemplifies the expansive problem with the mainstream media and how it serves as one of the primary instigators of racial division. Propaganda is extremely powerful. If you can find a way to control someone's emotions, you can control their thoughts and actions. It is not by accident that politicians regularly appeal to emotion. They want you to be emotional because when you are, it is difficult to be rational and you are easier to manipulate. Advertisers also do this because they know they can get people to buy their products if they are able to make them feel something.

What, then, is the predictable result of racially charged journalism? What is the intended outcome when these stories run? When the media shows you a video of a white teenager wearing a MAGA hat seemingly staring down a Native American man, what is the message they are trying to convey? Why would they not tell you the Native American man was the one who approached the teenager, got in his face, and began banging a drum and chanting? Why would they instead malign the teenager as a racist and say he was engaging in racial harassment?

What happens when they report that President Donald Trump called white supremacists "very fine people" without the full context of his remarks—which show that he actually outright condemned them? What could be the motive behind such intentional deception? What happens when they uncritically accept the outlandish story of

Jussie Smollett's attack and announce to viewers that this sort of hate crime is tragically "to be expected" in our racist country? What happens when mass shootings only get significant attention if the shooter is white? What happens when the media only mentions the race of alleged perpetrators of heinous crimes when the suspects are white? What happens when they only show video clips of white police officers shooting black suspects but omit the parts where the suspect fought the police and reached for a weapon? What do they expect to happen?

Why would the media declare that opposition to race-based instruction in elementary schools is due to white supremacy? Why do they only report on unarmed black suspects being killed by police while ignoring the much higher number of unarmed white suspects who are killed by police? What might that do to people's perceptions?

Why would they lie about Michael Brown having his hands up when police shot him in Ferguson, Missouri, in 2014? Why would they lie and say Jacob Blake was unarmed? Why would they call the BLM riots "mostly peaceful" even though more than thirty people were killed, including a child, and the rioters caused billions of dollars in damage?

The media has claimed that pushing back against COVID restrictions is racist. They have claimed that hiking is racist. They have claimed that roads are racist. Election laws, immigration laws, criticizing black athletes and entertainers, parents at school board meetings, the Academy Awards, the NFL combine, health care, guns, children's Halloween costumes, hairstyles, Band-Aids, the pro-life movement, the National Anthem, the Republican Party, the filibuster, Fox News, the entire state of Florida, the Founding Fathers, the Constitution, and often even America itself—the media has deemed all of these things to be racist. And that's just a very small percentage of the full list. If mainstream journalists truly believed in justice, particularly as it pertains to race, why would they do this?

There is a concept in psychology called the availability heuristic, which is a cognitive shortcut by which we analyze the likelihood of something occurring by relying on immediate examples that come to mind. This means that the more easily something is recalled, the more probable or common we think it is. The problem with this is that it's often inaccurate. To study this, in the 1970s, psychologists Daniel Kahnmen and Amos Tversky asked people to determine whether there are more words in the English language that begin with the letter K or more words that have K as their third letter. Seventy percent of the participants guessed that words beginning with K are more prevalent. In reality, twice as many words have K as the third letter. It is just much easier to think of words that begin with K, and that is what leads us to conclude that they are more common.[7]

Seeing how the availability heuristic can distort reality, it is easy to recognize how the media choosing to selectively report certain types of stories and injecting certain ideas into the public consciousness can play a major role in what the average person believes to be true. This is why people believe that Breonna Taylor, whom they falsely claim was shot by police while sleeping in her own apartment, is commonplace for black people, but what happened to Duncan Lemp—a white guy who was shot and killed by police during a similar no-knock raid—never happens. This is why people are so inclined to believe that a pull rope in a NASCAR garage is a noose meant for a black driver, that there is a high likelihood of two guys in MAGA hats attacking a black actor in Chicago, or that white supremacy is the greatest domestic threat facing the United States of America. This is why 75 percent of black Americans fear being attacked for their race by white people,[8] even though the truth is that at least 70 percent of interracial homicides are committed by black people killing white people.[9] People believe these things because this is the narrative that has been perpetuated by those we rely on to tell us the truth. They believe these things because the constant barrage of racism narratives, combined with selective reporting, are what most easily come to mind, not the actual facts.

So again, we must ask: why would the mainstream media do this? Are we supposed to believe they don't understand what the availability heuristic is and that they don't recognize the impact of their selective, skewed reporting, or what such biased journalism might do to people's perceptions of reality? There is a reason President Trump called them "the enemy of the people."

This should make it apparent that those who embrace and promote the lies of Critical Race Theory do not actually want to fix anything. They have no desire to solve racial problems. They need them—even if those problems need to be fabricated. Their identity, self-image, power, influence, and careers depend on perpetuating racial grievance. They have no interest in actual justice or even in the well-being of black people or other racial minorities. They are only interested in what can be exploited, what is currently politically expedient, what can help them maintain a career as a professional victim, and expanding the power and influence of their ideology.

This is why their focus is on vengeance instead of justice. They do not want the patient to get well.

CHAPTER 6

Diversity Is Our Strength?

*The worst forms of racial discrimination in this Nation
have always been accompanied by straight-faced representations that discrimination helped minorities.*

—U.S. Supreme Court Justice Clarence Thomas

How can you say you value diversity but oppose concepts like freedom of speech and diversity of thought? What is the point of diversity if no one is allowed to disagree or offer a "diverse" perspective? How can diversity be a strength if it relies on superficial and arbitrary filters and demands ideological conformity? What is the point in everyone looking different if everyone thinks the same?

Consider what might happen if a football team had only quarterbacks or only wide receivers. Would they win? Probably not. It is unlikely they would even be able to compete, as they could not function effectively as a team. This is true across most sports where team members play different positions that each require different skill sets, training regimens, body types, foot speeds, and strategies. These teams need diversity in order to fill these varied roles and work together as a cohesive unit. In this case, diversity is certainly an asset.

But what would happen if the football team diversified its positions but decided they needed a certain number of blue-eyed wide receivers or a certain percentage of players shorter than 5'8"? What if it limited the number of black players on the roster so as to provide a better racial balance? Would these decisions make the team stronger or weaker?

The quest for this idea of "diversity" has completely engulfed many of our institutions, with schools, universities, corporations, and even the government establishing entire departments with officers assigned to tackling the issue. The title "Diversity Officer" or "Chief Diversity Officer" has become commonplace. These departments help implement race-based policies aimed at bringing in more non-white employees, initiate "diversity" training, and pursue what they would call an "equitable work environment." That sounds fairly innocuous on its face, but as we have already discussed at length, words often have vastly different definitions in the progressive lexicon.

When CRT/antiracism advocates speak of diversity, they are not talking about the natural diversity we would see on a sports team. They are talking about a contrived, superficial diversity—and in this context, a superficial racial diversity. In other words, they pursue diversity for diversity's sake—making decisions about who to hire, who to promote, who to admit, and who to help based solely on race. In a sane world, that would be called "racism." Unfortunately, we do not live in a sane world any longer. Still, that's exactly what it is. It is not the diversity of quarterbacks and wide receivers filling their specialized roles to complete the needs of a team; it is the diversity of selecting quarterbacks and wide receivers based on superficial and arbitrary qualifiers that have nothing to do with the position they are playing.

Superficial diversity and superficial uniformity are two sides of the same coin. Both are driven by twisted logic, and both involve the dismissal of better, stronger options for the sake of fulfilling some arbitrary objective. Focusing on things that have nothing to do with what the particular task requires inevitably leads to inferior outcomes.

Perhaps we make white players' baskets worth more points and let them have open shots. Maybe we allow teams to field six players instead of five if they have a white person on the court. Maybe we penalize teams for not having enough white players by excluding them from the playoffs until they recruit more of them. Do you see the flaws in the logic? How embarrassing and insulting would that be for the white players? How unfair would it be for the black players?

What is the difference?

No one questions the merit-based outcomes of the NBA, even though its racial makeup is heavily skewed and nowhere near representative of the general population. But if the races are reversed, suddenly we have a problem that requires aggressive intervention and manipulation of outcomes.

The entire approach to diversity is abhorrent and nothing more than a continuation of the very problems it claims to be trying to fix. Just as it would be clearly foolish to try to balance the NBA by signing more white players and excluding black players, it would be equally foolish to include black players just because they are black and not based on their exceptional skill as a basketball player. This is true no matter where it happens—whether on the basketball court or at the U.S. Supreme Court. Such behavior still perpetuates racism and entirely misses the point of diversity. The pendulum has only swung in the opposite direction. It was not, and never should have been, about simply including black or other non-white people in all areas of our society. It should be about removing race as a variable altogether, focusing instead on merit and skill sets, not skin color. Diversity is a byproduct of removing race as a variable, not the lever by which you manipulate outcomes.

This distinction is critical. The logic underlying affirmative action programs should offend anyone who cares to examine it. In *Fisher v. University of Texas* (2013), Supreme Court Justice Clarence Thomas strongly reinforced this view by stating that "the pursuit of diversity as an end is nothing more than impermissible 'racial balancing.'" He called it "a badge of inferiority" and said such practices "taint the accomplishments of all those who are admitted on the basis of racial discrimination." He wrote,

> It is an open question whether their skin color played a part in their advancement. The question itself is the stigma—because either racial discrimination did play a role, in which case the person may be deemed "otherwise unqualified," or it did not, in which case asking the question itself unfairly marks those who would succeed without discrimination.[2]

This is exactly correct. Any time a black person succeeds in such an environment, there will always be the question of whether their achievement was attained by their merit or by their race. There will always be an asterisk beside their name. If they are qualified, then they don't need affirmative action to succeed.

In the same case, Thomas also pointed out that the behavior and arguments used to justify racial discrimination in favor of blacks are no different from the rationalizations surrounding racial segregation in the 1950s (e.g., that it would provide more opportunities for black leaders) and even arguments held by pro-slavery advocates (e.g., that it is a positive, moral good that elevates blacks). Those arguments were eventually struck down by the Supreme Court and wholly rejected as any sort of justification for discriminating on the basis of race. Thomas went on to proclaim that the Equal Protection Clause of the Fourteenth Amendment demands that "all applicants must be treated equally under the law, and no benefit in the eye of the beholder can justify racial discrimination" and that "the worst forms of racial discrimination in this Nation have always been accompanied by straight-faced representations that discrimination helped minorities."[3]

The idea that black people or other minorities should be *given* opportunities rather than that they possess the ability to earn them should absolutely be considered racist, and affirmative action should be seen as the immoral, unconstitutional practice that it is. It is a kind of racial charity passed down from progressive white saviors to the poor, lowly Negro who cannot succeed without their help. How can he get a degree from a university unless he is given preference and his test scores are ignored? How can he get a job unless he is given special consideration and accommodations? How can he succeed unless white people lift him up on their shoulders? This is the attitude behind diversity, equity, and inclusion initiatives. It is unequivocally racist at its core. This bigotry of low expectations thrives in the progressive notions of diversity.

The Progressive Bubble

The push for so-called diversity in academia, in Hollywood, in corporate settings, etc., is nothing more than a call for condescending pity prizes cloaked in performative benevolence for the sake of virtue signaling. That's ultimately what this is about. It's not truly about the people. It's not truly about disparities or injustice. It's about social credit, and it's about power. What does Harvard University gain from shutting out the most intelligent, best-performing applicants in favor of poorer-performing applicants? It gains social credit and maybe, more importantly, avoids losing it. Asian-Americans are considered white-adjacent in the Critical Race Theory fantasy world and, therefore, it is acceptable to discriminate against them as well as whites in favor of other races in the college application process. By engaging in such discrimination, schools like Harvard make it clear that they are not concerned with diversity. They are only concerned with signaling their commitment to progressive dogma. For those who embrace CRT ideology and wear the badge of antiracism, whatever gives them more power or paves the road toward gaining it is what they will do—even if it contradicts what they claimed to believe yesterday. Even if they were saying #StopAsianHate one minute, they will support rejecting applicants based solely on their Asian heritage the next.

Those who promote "diversity" and "inclusion" do not seem to actually care about these concepts. Rather, they are merely a means to an end. Consider what happened at Arizona State University in late 2021, when two white students were confronted by black students for the crimes of being white, supporting police, and sitting in the multicultural center. The black students filmed the interaction, accusing the white students of racism and telling them they needed to leave because they were not welcome in a "multicultural space."[4] Seemingly, what diversity, equity, and inclusion meant was there were "no white people allowed."

When television shows or movies feature non-white casts, progressives celebrate them for their diversity. When a company announces its leadership is completely run by minorities, it is celebrated for its diversity. If a government program is run by non-white people, it is, again, celebrated for its diversity. Let any of those things be all-white, though, and suddenly there is a significant problem to address. There appears to be a theme here.

This so-called "diversity" includes a demand for ideological conformity. The word "diversity" seems to also mean "no conservatives" or "nothing that challenges progressivism." Otherwise, why would universities that brand themselves as champions of diversity and inclusion shut down the events of conservative speakers? Why would they oppose having someone like Ben Shapiro come on campus to speak?

Why would the students at these universities shout down speakers they disagree with and attempt to disrupt their events? Why would some students believe that resorting to violence is acceptable to silence someone you disagree with? How is that pursuing diversity?

The Foundation for Individual Rights in Education (FIRE), along with RealClearEducation and College Pulse, conducted a survey in 2021 that showed 66 percent of college students supported shouting down speakers they don't agree with, and 23 percent supported using violence to shut down a speech event.[5] These numbers illustrate the expanding problem of intolerance for differing viewpoints that exists, not just on university campuses, but in workplaces, on social media, and all throughout our society. There is this idea that disagreeing with progressive ideology is akin to literal violence and therefore, can and should be met with the strongest opposition, which includes censorship, bans, and sometimes even actual violence. Diversity can only truly exist so far as it lives within the progressive framework. Everything else must be expunged.

As mentioned previously, Critical Race Theory is extremely hostile toward the First Amendment and the idea of free speech. CRT advocates and progressives in general believe that speech is used as a tool for oppression, and speech that goes against what they deem to be the correct ideology puts lives in danger and therefore must be silenced. When a white supremacist committed a mass shooting at a supermarket in Buffalo, New York, in May 2022,[6] progressives leapt into action, saying conservative speech led to the shooting (never mind the fact that the shooter explicitly denounced conservatism in his manifesto). However, no such analysis occurred after a black supremacist committed a mass shooting on a New York subway just a few days earlier[7] or when a black supremacist in Wisconsin ran over multiple white people with his car at a Christmas parade in late 2021.[8] No such analysis occurred when a Bernie Sanders supporter and

Rachel Maddow enthusiast attempted to assassinate Republican members of Congress at a baseball game in 2017, nearly murdering Rep. Steve Scalise.[9] No such analysis occurred when a man who was upset about *Roe v. Wade* being overturned in mid-2022 attempted to assassinate Supreme Court Justice Brett Kavanaugh.[10] There was no talk of dangerous rhetoric leading up to any of it, or words being akin to violence.

A common tactic of the political left has been to label the speech of their opponents as "hate speech" and then label the people, themselves, as having some kind of "-ism" or "phobia." Antifa regularly equates conservatives with Nazis ("Punch a Nazi" was a fashionable phrase around the time Trump was elected in 2016) and determines that those with such violence-inciting ideas deserve a violent response, all in the name of fighting fascism. This tactic does a couple of things: It reduces their opponents to evil, dangerous creatures instead of human beings, which means that they don't have to contend with the merit of their opponents' ideas or listen to anything they have to say. It also gives them permission and moral justification to essentially do whatever they want to them, including violently attacking them, which Antifa has done and continues to do. Equating words with violence means that words can be punished like violence and words also can be met with violence.

What this ultimately means is that these ideas of "diversity" can only truly exist within the progressive bubble. Diversity of thought and opinions are not permitted to extend beyond that bubble. This is why the ratio of progressive to conservative professors on college campuses is 12:1.[11] This is why when Apple runs a campaign to "promote black voices," you will find zero black conservative voices in that group. This is why a room full of white people from different countries, different cultures, and who speak different languages would somehow be considered less diverse than a room full of black people who are all from the same neighborhood. "Diversity" is wholly dependent on progressive ideology.

Subtext

It is not uncommon to find opposition to interracial relationships and interracial marriage (known as anti-miscegenation) among those who adhere to CRT. They very much agree with the grandfather of the little girl who stopped talking to my son—white people should be with white people and black people should be with black people. There was substantial backlash against Lebron James's son taking a girl who happened to be white to prom, as if it were some form of racial betrayal or he was fraternizing with the enemy.[12] Social media is full of people with the terms "antiracism" or "Black Lives Matter" in their bios who espouse hateful views against "mixed" couples. I have personally been criticized by race activists for not marrying a "fully black" woman (whatever that means). Even people who don't know who my wife is have made quips like, "He must be married to a white woman." Is that a quest for diversity?

It is also common to see "antiracists" vehemently opposing white families seeking to adopt non-white children. These families are accused of being naïve and privileged at best, or fetishizers and abusers at worst. Does that sound like a quest for diversity?

Race activists regularly denigrate white people and attack their character, not for anything they have actually done, but simply for being white. For example, forensic psychiatrist and Yale lecturer Aruna Khilanani said in an interview that all white people are racist, that there are no good apples among them, that white people are psychopathic, and that she fantasizes about shooting them.[13] She received support from people like writer Imani Bashir, who tweeted of Khilanai's tirade,

She isn't totally off here. You're talking about a people who have globally raped, pillaged, murdered, and still to this very day. Any other group is judged off one or two past possible offenses in their own lifetime, let alone multiple generations, and it's time we call a spade a spade![14]

Likewise, University of Washington political science professor Megan Ming Francis told a Ted Talk audience, "The problem isn't just a few bad apples. The problem is that the whole tree is infected."[15]

Does this sound like they are seeking diversity or racial harmony? White people are regularly told they are not allowed to have outspoken opinions on racism or any racial issues—that they must remain silent in black spaces and do nothing but listen and learn. This kind of rhetoric is present in corporate training seminars on antiracism: White employees must be silent and take this kind of verbal abuse from people like Khilanani and Francis. How does that pursue diversity? Unless, of course, diversity means, "Shut up and bend the knee to my ideology."

The type of diversity progressivism and Critical Race Theory call for is merely a tactical tool meant to further the goals of the ideology. That's it. When advocates say, "Diversity is our strength," they are talking about capitulation and conformity, not diversity. In other words, they don't want strength at all; they want weakness. They want people to be powerless and easily controlled. Their idea of "strength" is nothing more than expansion of their own power and control. All we need to do is give them more power, and everything will be wonderful.

Once again, we see that the meaning behind the words being used is something entirely different from what is stated. Diversity actually means ideological conformity, inclusion actually means ideological exclusion, and equity actually means ideological inequity.

In theatre, we often talk of subtext, which is what a particular character means to say rather than what they actually say. A character could say "I love you," but the subtext of the line might be, "I hate your guts." If we only have the written line and no other information, we will accept the surface-level meaning and assume that the character is expressing some deep affection for another. However, knowing the subtext changes the line completely; it changes the entire context of the scene and changes how the line is delivered, the motivations and intentions, the actor's body language, subsequent character actions, tactics, prop usage, etc. This is what we are dealing with when it comes to deceptive concepts like "diversity." The written line is "I love you," but the subtext is "I hate your guts."

CHAPTER 7

Inclusion and Compassion, but Not for You

It's a big, bright beautiful world—but not for you.

—Shrek's parents, *Shrek: The Musical*

Tolerance. Compassion. Empathy. How often have we heard these words? We are regularly lectured by our moral betters about the importance of tolerating the cultures and perspectives of those who are different from us, about having compassion and empathy for others who look and act differently than we do—yet all the while, these same people refuse to tolerate or show compassion for anyone or anything that challenges their dogma. Those who embrace the tenets of Critical Race Theory and antiracism claim to be much more empathetic and compassionate than everyone else and lean on these concepts to promote policies and practices that are neither empathetic nor compassionate. Just as with the idea of diversity, the concepts of inclusion, empathy, and compassion are all entirely based on ideology.

In the opening scene of *Shrek: The Musical*, we see a young ogre named Shrek being kicked out of his home and sent off to live on his own on his seventh birthday. His parents sing happily about how wonderful and magical the world is, but then remind the young ogre that he does not get to partake in that version of it. His world is going to be dark and gloomy, and he is destined to live in the swampy shadows. The bubbly chorus describes their belief that the world is a "big, bright, beautiful" place where "every dream comes true—but not for you,"[1] setting the young ogre's expectations for his own life at the lowest possible level.

Shrek's parents are full of empathy and compassion—or at least they believe they are. They know that the world is going to be hard on young Shrek and they want him to be prepared for it. But there is a clear disconnect between these feelings (which any parent would share) and their actions. They demonstrate their love, empathy, and compassion by kicking a seven-year-old child out of their house and forcing him to survive on his own. Something is obviously missing in the execution here.

In a parallel scene, Princess Fiona is also subjected to the "empathy" of her parents who "compassionately" lock her away in a tower on Christmas Eve; she will be forced to remain there for twenty years to protect her from herself. Like Shrek's parents, Fiona's also demonstrate a disconnect between feelings of compassion and the actions they take to demonstrate it.

Clearly, this is an outrageous fairy tale, and these things are meant to be comedic in their exaggerated awfulness. However, they do demonstrate something important about the idea of empathy and what qualifies as compassion in action, which I think is worth exploring in the context of progressivism and Critical Race Theory.

Most people would agree that it is not compassionate to allow your children to play in a busy street. It is obvious that such behavior would be negligent and place your children's lives in danger. Most people would also agree that it is sadistic, not compassionate, to enjoy your children being upset and intentionally trying to make them cry. What kind of parent would want their children to be hurt or upset?

But with these things in mind, what happens when your child gets upset and cries because they want to play in a busy street? What is the compassionate response?

Remember our example from Chapter 4—the child who wants to eat candy for breakfast? Wouldn't the compassionate response be to allow him to do so in order to demonstrate that you love him and want him to be happy?

On the other end of the spectrum, overprotective parents would never let their children do anything at all for fear that they might get hurt. They are engulfed by the belief that children should not be exposed to any risk whatsoever in order to protect them. But this hinders them from developing any independence, as they are basically confined to a protective bubble for their entire childhood. The parents believe this is the compassionate response. They never recognize that in attempting to avoid harm, they are actually harming their children themselves.

If we look at Critical Race Theory and progressivism at large, we can see how they embrace both extremes. They allow children to play in that busy street to keep them from crying, while they also demand children remain encased in a protective emotional bubble, never being exposed to anything that might hurt their feelings. These are the kind of thought processes that underlie expressions of "empathy." (Of course, I say that, and a year from now there will be articles in the *Washington Post* under the headline, "Why Not Allowing Your Children to Play in Traffic Is Indicative of Whiteness" or "The Racist History of the Word 'Overprotective.'") Regardless, when it comes to expressions of empathy, whatever potential long-term harm exists and whatever second- or third-order effects that may surface down the line are ignored in favor of short-term, myopic expressions of "Look how much we care." This is clearly seen in Critical Race Theory ideology in that its proponents want children protected from contrived concepts like microaggressions and demand that they never be exposed to the horrors of racism that lie within behavior like inadvertently mispronouncing someone's name. They also want to be sure to instill guilt in some children for things they didn't do and victimhood in others for things they didn't experience. We also see this in areas like gender discussions, where using the wrong pronoun can send a person into a meltdown and where young children are allowed to make life-altering decisions about puberty blockers and sometimes even surgery so that they can live as the opposite gender. (My daughters often believe they are unicorns. Apparently, it would be compassionate for me and my wife to refer to them with unicorn pronouns, to surgically install horns into their foreheads, and then send them outside to live in a barn.)

This is what happens when you are driven by emotion and not by reason. Well-known psychologist, author, and lecturer Jordan Peterson often talks about how reflexive empathy is not actually a virtue. He points out that compassion for infants and elderly people who can't take care of themselves is great, but it can be devastating for others if not tempered. Empathy can't just be unbridled. He likes to say, "You have to think. You can't just feel."[2] Allowing children to do anything they want without regard for how such actions will affect their long-term well-being and safety will have devastating effects on their growth and development as human beings. Continually treating anyone, let alone children, like helpless victims will do the same.

I have worked as a speech-language pathologist for almost ten years now. I currently work at a skilled nursing facility in Ohio, and one of my duties is helping rehabilitate dementia and stroke patients. This often means helping them with their speech, their memory, their thought organization, and their eating. One of the things you learn when working in a rehabilitation environment is that you must work to facilitate independence—and you do that by encouraging the patient to do as much on their own as possible. You avoid doing things for them that they can do themselves, even if it means they have to struggle to do them. If I have a stroke patient who has difficulty bringing her fork to her mouth, I would not actually be helping her by taking the fork away and feeding her. That doesn't mean I like watching her struggle or that I want things to be more difficult for her, but I know that if I don't allow her to fight through and do it on her own, she will never get her independence back. Compassion makes me want to help her accomplish the task. It makes me not want to see her struggle. I feel bad for her and don't want her to go through such an ordeal. But reason keeps me from acting on those feelings of compassion because I know that if I do, the result will be worse, and I will do even more harm to her. Now, that doesn't mean I act like Shrek's parents and throw her out into the world to fend for herself without any assistance whatsoever, but it does mean that I recognize that she needs to do some things on her own to regain her overall function.

An iconic scene from *Finding Nemo* comes to mind. A fish named Gill, who is a leader in his fish tank, refuses to save Nemo when he is sucked into the filter tube. Nemo begs for assistance, and the other fish panic as they rush to help him, but Gill—in his calm, collected voice—says, "Nobody touch him."[3] Gill tells Nemo he has the ability to swim out on his own, to which Nemo replies that he can't because he has a bad fin. This is a critical moment because Nemo has offered a plausible excuse for why he can't succeed, why he needs to be dependent, and why he is a victim. Gill could give in to compassion here, affirm Nemo's victimhood, and help him out of the tube. Who wants to see a young fish with a bad fin struggle like that? It's cruel! Heartless! Don't you care?! But Gill doesn't do that. Gill sees that Nemo has the power to overcome his obstacles and knows that by allowing him to do it on his own, he will crush that victim mentality and help

Nemo realize his own strength. By doing so, Gill shows that he is the most compassionate of any fish in that tank.

This is one of my biggest issues with the continued victim hustling of race-based ideology, particularly how it targets and impacts innocent children. First, its advocates sell you the disease and convince you that you, too, are stuck in a filter tube because you are a victim of injustice. Just look at your gimpy fin! The only reason you are in the filter tube in the first place is because someone else put you there! You are oppressed!

They will then sell you the snake-oil cure, rejecting any notion that you have the strength and capability to swim out on your own. They will be offended by the mere suggestion that you should try. (Gill would be reprimanded for suggesting such a thing and sent to cultural sensitivity training for harmful microaggressions.) You can't swim out on your own, and besides, it's some other fish's fault you have a bad fin, and the only way for you to get out of the tube is to embrace filter justice. You must demand equity. Demand that those other fish over there acknowledge their privilege of not being stuck in a filter and deconstruct their fishness. They must also maim their own fins to demonstrate that they are allies! Of course, none of this ever works. You just stay stuck, and now everyone in the tank has a gimpy fin and hates each other—well, except for the hustlers. They get rich and retire to the ocean, leaving you stuck in a fish tank filter.

There is a concept in psychology called "learned helplessness." Psychologists Martin Seligman and Steven Maier coined the term when they discovered during their research that dogs placed in a shuttle box would stop trying to avoid a shock to their back paws when they "learned" they could do nothing to escape it. Even when it was possible to escape the shock by jumping over a barrier, the dogs refused to try. They merely accepted their circumstances and assumed they were helpless.[4] This tragic phenomenon occurs in humans as well, as people develop an external locus of control and stop trying. Is it compassionate to teach children to feel helpless?

Emotional reasoning is almost always faulty when not tempered by reason. Our emotions are not always reliable indicators of truth and reality, especially in the absence of evidence. Simply feeling like something is true doesn't mean that it is. You may feel like racism is woven into the fabric of our society, but that doesn't make it true. You may feel like you are a different gender than the one you were born with, but that doesn't make it true. Emotions cannot rule these discussions. Compassion not tempered by reason is not compassion at all.

Misguided Compassion of Fictional Villains

Fictional villains are often great examples of misguided compassion. The mark of a great villain is one who truly believes that he is doing good. He believes he is the hero of the story. This is true for real-life villains as well. The greatest evils throughout history have been committed in the name of compassion and self-proclaimed devotion to unblemished morality, often with millions of supporters behind the people leading the charge . . . who eventually leave millions of dead bodies in their wake. Hitler, Stalin, Lenin, Mao, Pol Pot, Mussolini, Idi Amin—they all believed themselves to be morally justified in their actions, and yet they were the direct cause of unimaginable horrors. We can and should learn from history, but I find that fiction is a powerful tool for bringing out reality. As Pablo Picasso once said, "Art is a lie that makes us realize truth."

Consider a Marvel Cinematic Universe villain like Thanos. In *Avengers: Infinity War*, Thanos seeks to provide balance to the universe, believing that if he doesn't, there will be overpopulation and resource shortages which will lead to mass suffering and death.[5] On its face, this is the noble quest of a hero. Thanos's solution, however, is to use the Infinity Stones to randomly wipe out half of the population in the universe. He certainly believes he is being guided by compassion. The problem is that he lacks reason and believes that his ends justify his abhorrent means.

In *Avatar: The Last Airbender*, Fire Lord Sozin believes the Fire Nation is blessed with peace and prosperity and that it should spread to the rest of the world.[6] Again, it is noble to want the world to share in your blessings. But Sozin's solution is to start a war and conquer the other nations by force, committing genocide against the Air Nomads in the process.

In the world of *Harry Potter*, we discover that Dumbledore and Grindelwald once planned to seek out the Deathly Hallows to rule over the non-magical Muggles, believing this would make a peaceful world for all. Dumbledore eventually came to his senses. Grindelwald, however, continued with his "compassionate" plans, leading him to become a powerful and murderous dark wizard who caused widespread death and destruction.[7]

Another good *Harry Potter* example is the insufferable government bureaucrat and teacher Dolores Umbridge. She believes completely in the authority and infallibility of the Ministry of Magic, and she believes in power. She is such an awful villain that it is difficult to believe she isn't in league with Voldemort himself. But again, she is so driven by thinking she is acting "for the greater good" that she is willing to do whatever is required to achieve her goals. In a particularly revealing moment, she talks herself into using the illegal Cruciatus Curse on Harry—a curse which causes immense pain—in order to get him to tell her what she wants to know. She believes it is "an issue of Ministry security" and "school discipline."[8] She believes hers is the noble course of action.

How about Anakin Skywalker, who will eventually become Darth Vader, in *Star Wars*? He is entirely motivated by a desire to keep the woman he loves from dying, at any cost. Protecting the people you love is clearly admirable, but Anakin chooses the wrong path to do it—a path that leads him to the Dark Side and ultimately leads to the very thing he fears the most: Padme's death.[9] Anakin makes a deal with the devil to try to do what he believes is right and ends up destroying everything he loves, as well as himself.

One final example is Inspector Javert in *Les Misérables*. Javert is wholly dedicated to the law and willing to do anything to protect its sanctity. In his eyes, Jean Valjean can never change. He believes Valjean is and always will be a degenerate criminal who deserves to rot in prison. Javert hunts Valjean and attempts to do whatever he can to see him sent back to prison, even though Valjean is now living an honest, law-abiding life. When Valjean repeatedly commits good deeds and ultimately spares Javert's life when he has an opportunity to take it, Javert experiences an identity crisis that ultimately leads him to commit suicide.[10]

Like the villains in these stories, people never see themselves as being the villain—they see themselves as noble heroes. And like the fictional villains, they often believe that their good intentions are all that matter, that their goals are the only relevant criteria to consider, and that as long as something is done "for the greater good," it justifies the methods used to achieve it. Good intentions receive all the spotlight while tactics and actual outcomes are ignored. All that matters is the surface-level analysis and how it makes people feel. This is why federal bills are given flowery names that no one would disagree with. "How can something called 'The American Rescue Plan' be problematic? You don't want Americans to be rescued?!" This is the state of our national discourse and analysis. Too often, emotion-laden "the end justifies the means" thinking rules the world of politics and policy. And "for the greater good" is almost always a preface for some evil about to be inflicted on the populace.

Feel-good rhetoric about the intentions of a government policy almost never equates to that policy doing what it claims to do. As we have already seen, advocates of DEI policies claim it will do all kinds of things, like reduce racism, teach true history, create equitable environments, etc. In reality, they don't do any of those things. Instead, they perpetuate racism and deepen racial division, teach a false and skewed history through the lens of race, openly discriminate based on race in the name of diversity and equity, and divide everyone into groups of victims and oppressors. None of that matters to ideologues, though. What's important is that they believe their intentions are driven by compassion and empathy, or at least that you believe it.

Thomas Sowell famously said, "Liberals seem to assume that, if you don't believe in their particular political solutions, then you don't really care about the people that they claim to want to help."[11] This is an accurate and insightful assessment of the problem. Such behavior is, yet again, nothing more than an appeal to emotion. It is a demand for emotional reasoning. Your support (or lack thereof) of a given policy indicates your level of supposed compassion. If you don't support that particular policy or position, you are a heartless bigot with no compassion or empathy for other human beings. There is no regard for perspectives that include different solutions. Many people have dismissed me for my opposition to some leftist policy by saying, "I can't make you care about other people"—as if my opposition to expansive government power and control means I want people to suffer.

In order to demonstrate my empathy in the world of progressivism, I must accept that my children are victims of oppression and treat them as such, I must accept that my white friends and family members are all oppressors and complicit with systems of white supremacy, and I must allow strangers to teach my children to obsess over race and view everything through a victim/oppressor dichotomy, or else I do not care about them. If I refuse, I have no compassion and no empathy.

Inclusion by Exclusion

Another element of this is the rationale behind the idea of inclusivity. Again, there is that claim that feeling empathy and compassion drives the desire to be inclusive. Like all of these ideas, it looks acceptable on the surface, like something any reasonable person would agree with. Of course, we want to be inclusive. We don't want to exclude people on the basis of race, gender, or anything else. We want to be kind to others and not treat them badly, especially based on things they can't control. But once again, the underlying subtext is something entirely different than the written line.

We see a couple of different things here. One is a quest for inclusivity that involves completely erasing established definitions, categories, and common sense. For example, women are called "breeders" or "birthing people" in order to include transgender people. We are compelled to abandon English pronouns and use nonsensical pronouns like *ze* and *zir* to accommodate those who consider themselves to be "nonbinary." Children must be made to read books like *Antiracist Baby*, and their parents must pretend it's completely normal to instill children with a victim mentality or teach them that their skin color confers privilege. We have to pretend terms like "master bedroom" and "blacklist" are offensive to black people and need to be changed in order to be more racially and culturally inclusive. It's nonsense.

The other aspect of this "inclusivity" is actually the complete opposite of inclusion: anyone who is labeled a heretic of the religion of wokeness is blatantly excluded. There is no concern for the feelings, perspectives, or cultural differences of the people who disagree with progressivism. All talk of tolerance and inclusivity goes right out the window. Like the idea of diversity, the idea of inclusion depends wholly on whether one falls within the boundaries of acceptable progressive thought.

The logic driving all of this is that it is compassionate to include victims of oppression and exclude their oppressors. The ideology of progressivism determines who gets labeled a victim or an oppressor. This can change on a moment-by-moment basis. One moment, it may be black people atop the victimhood hierarchy, the next moment it may be Muslims, the next it may be trans people, the next moment it may be women. It wholly depends on what is politically expedient at the time. Everything is fluid.

While gender madness is not really within the purview of this book, it is not unrelated to race madness. It is difficult to speak about Critical Race Theory without also mentioning gender and queer theory. The underlying pathology I'm referring to here drives both. One thing I find interesting about this supposed quest for inclusivity is how it continues to expand the design of the LGBT flag to the point where it is essentially meaningless. Activists continue to add letters to the acronym—so many that almost no one can even remember the latest order, let alone what each letter stands for. New flags with new designs are continually added, and even people who support the movement struggle to remember what they all mean. Progressives apparently feel the umbrella is too broad, so they find new ways to describe themselves. There is no longer just one pride flag; there are at least twenty. It's no longer "LGBT." It's "LGBTQIA+." And I'm sure all of that will probably be outdated and considered bigoted and problematic by the time this book is published.

A similar phenomenon happens in the realm of race. People fracture themselves into various racial subgroups under a larger umbrella so as to claim some kind of exclusive identity. This is wholly ironic, given the fact that they simultaneously claim to be pursuing inclusivity. But you will find that "black people" is no longer an acceptable term for many, and a term like BIPOC, which stands for "Black, Indigenous, and People of Color" is utterly offensive. Why? Because it's *too* inclusive. The black people who demand inclusivity in society often hate being placed in broad, inclusive categories. They splinter themselves into groups like "FBA," which stands for Foundational Black Americans, or "ADOS," which stands for American Descendants of Slavery, to distinguish themselves from other so-called black people. They will make distinctions between being physically black, being culturally black, and being politically black. Black people from other countries are not accepted in the same category of black people from America. Everyone wants to take their ball and go home.

This kind of fracturing is to be expected in groups that consider victimhood and the subsequent fight against oppression to be the highest of moral virtues. Predictably, the supposed victims will attempt to out-victimize each other. This behavior is incentivized and socially reinforced. You will see this happen frequently across self-proclaimed marginalized groups as they battle it out in the Oppression Olympics to determine which of them is the most oppressed.

What is fascinating about such behavior is how close it comes to recognizing and embracing individualism. At their core, these ideologies are inherently collectivist. They all elevate the group above the individual. It is all about group rights and "the greater good." Everything must be organized into communities—the black community, the LGBT community, etc. But what happens with this splintering is the individuals begin to recognize that the broad group does not represent them perfectly and does not always have their best interests at heart. They begin to want their individualism to shine through. So they create new, much narrower categories for themselves—categories that include far fewer people (i.e., intentional exclusion). This splintering could feasibly continue indefinitely, creating narrower and narrower categories until finally, it is reduced to a single person: the individual. I personally identify as an FMA—Foundational Mocha American. My pronouns are leave/me/alone. Do I get my own flag?

Doublethink

A common theme within progressivism and its sub-ideologies like gender theory, queer theory, and Critical Race Theory is something George Orwell called "doublethink." In his book *Nineteen Eighty-Four*, he describes it as "the power to hold two contradictory beliefs in one's mind simultaneously and accept both of them."[12] There are many examples of this. Whether it's ideas on democracy, norms, antiharassment, antiviolence, bodily autonomy, the word "woman," police power, etc.—you will find progressivism taking opposite positions at different times based on what is advantageous in the moment. If you zoom out, you can see it applies broadly to the stated importance of compassion and empathy that underlies so much of what drives the ideology. These are the primary weapons, so compassion and empathy are used to explain away the doublethink. Sometimes it is compassionate to treat people like individual human beings and not a racial collective. Other times, it is compassionate to attack or malign people for their race. Sometimes it is compassionate to embrace the uniqueness, strength, and power of being a woman. Other times, it is compassionate to pretend you can't even define what a woman is. Sometimes it is compassionate to claim that speech is violence. Other times it is compassionate to claim that violence is speech. Compassion, therefore, is contingent on whether someone agrees with one's political views.

Those who oppose CRT need to understand that its advocates believe it is compassionate to stand against racism and also to group people into collectives based on race while assigning value judgments to each group in the name of progressive causes. It is, therefore, compassionate to stand against racism while engaging in it. Critical Race Theory advocates believe it is compassionate to empower others, but also to infuse children with a victimhood mentality and learned helplessness. Critical Race Theory advocates believe it is compassionate to unify people, but also to divide people into victims and oppressors and pit them against each other. Critical Race Theory advocates are wholly empathetic—just not when someone disagrees with its claims. Critical Race Theory advocates embrace inclusion and compassion—just not for you.

CHAPTER 8

Equity Is the Opposite of Equality

The smallest minority on Earth is the individual.

—Ayn Rand

What is equity? At a glance, it seems like a fairly innocuous word. It kind of looks and sounds like the word "equality," so surely it can't be all that bad. When people claim to want racial equity, don't they just mean they want everyone to be treated equally? Wasn't that the ultimate goal of the civil rights movement and Dr. Martin Luther King?

Those who push principles of equity definitely want us to believe these things. They use a word that suggests a relationship with equality on purpose to obscure what equity truly means and what their goals actually are. Oftentimes, equity is even marketed as a replacement for equality, with "equality" being treated like an old piece of worn-out, racist machinery that needs to be replaced by the shiny and trendy new word.

A popular graphic passed around on social media explains the basic concept behind equity. It is an image of three people of different heights behind a fence watching a baseball game. The tallest person can see over the fence just fine. The next person, who is shorter, needs a box to stand on to see over the fence. The shortest person needs two boxes in order to see. The message is that equity is treating people differently based on their specific needs so that they may achieve equal outcomes.

Once again, this does not seem too nefarious in theory. Clearly, people are different, and one size does not fit all. That much is true, and most people would agree on it. However, the way this manifests is the problem. In practice, it yields a sort of zero-sum approach, where one person must lose something for the other person to gain. The fact that the other two people are taller than the shortest person is determined to be unfair. To remedy this, taller people must be punished in some manner for their tallness, and their privilege must be erased to equalize the situation. Here, that might mean the taller people must have their legs cut off so that everyone ends up on the same level and no one can see the game. It's a bit morbid, but the point remains. As Karl Marx taught, "From each according to his ability, to each according to his needs"—equity inherently means deliberately unequal and discriminatory treatment in pursuit of some utopian vision of equal outcomes.

But equity is incapable of lifting anyone up. It can only tear people down.

Ayn Rand demonstrated this in *The Return of the Primitive: The Anti-Industrial Revolution*. She wrote,

> To understand the meaning and motives of egalitarianism, project it into the field of medicine. Suppose a doctor is called to help a man with a broken leg and, instead of setting it, proceeds to break the legs of ten other men, explaining that this would make the patient feel better; when all these men become crippled for life, the doctor advocates for the passage of a law compelling everyone to

walk on crutches—in order to make the cripples feel better
and equalize the "unfairness" of nature. If this is unspeak-
able, how does it acquire an aura of morality—or even the
benefit of a moral doubt—when practiced in regard to
man's mind?[1]

The point is that it is not at all possible to equalize the infinite
variables that combine in an infinite array of combinations to create
each individual. It cannot be done. As Rand says, "Nature does not
endow all men with equal beauty or equal intelligence and the faculty
of volition leads men to make different choices." This means that in
order to achieve equal outcomes, you need to somehow get rid of
nature and free will. This is the description of a dictatorship. Only
through tyranny can you even attempt to accomplish such a thing. It
is one thing to promote egalitarianism in the context of equality
before the law, but quite another to attempt to establish equality of
outcomes by force.

The other problem is how any of this even gets analyzed. Someone
having an advantage over another person because he is taller and can
therefore see over a fence is observable and quantifiable. But what if
they are both the same height and their differences are merely racial?
How does one determine the level of privilege in such a scenario, let
alone use it to attempt to manipulate outcomes? That isn't even mentioning that such a practice would be clear racial discrimination and
wholly unethical, even if you could somehow quantify it.

Additionally, such analyses always work from a position that
"white" is equal to privilege, so what would such an analysis look
like when comparing someone like Lebron James to a random
white person living in poverty somewhere in Appalachia? How
would someone pursuing racial equity even begin to analyze such
a scenario? Wouldn't true equity see Lebron hampered and the

impoverished white person lifted up? Shouldn't Lebron be made to share his immense wealth with those white people in southeastern Ohio who are less fortunate than him? Shouldn't the professional sports system that yields such tremendous disparities in income be dismantled in favor of closing that equity gap? None of it makes any sense in practice.

In Kurt Vonnegut's short story *Harrison Bergeron*, everyone in society is made to be completely equal. That means no one can be more attractive, more intelligent, or more physically skilled than anyone else. In order to accomplish this, the people who are more attractive, intelligent, and physically skilled are forced by the government to be handicapped in some manner. Harrison's dad is made to wear a radio in his ear that regulates his above-average intelligence. Ballerinas have to wear heavy weights to impede their superior physical abilities as well as to wear masks to hide their beauty. People with pleasant voices have to speak in unattractive tones so no one else will feel bad about their own voice.[2]

This is equity in action. The notion is that when some people have better outcomes than others, it indicates some form of group-level oppression is at work, so everything must be manipulated and equalized. That's why if more white children excel in math than black children, instead of helping the children who struggle with math improve their ability to grasp the concepts and increase their time spent on homework, math is deemed racist and unfair. White students are told that math is a system that was made for them, which means they are somehow to blame for the struggling black student, even if the white student also is struggling with it. As a result, the entire approach to mathematics is altered to accommodate the underperforming black students, and the white students must be made aware of their unearned privilege regardless of whether they are actually doing well in math.

Too many black students scoring low on standardized testing? The solution is not to help those students improve their scores, but to get rid of standardized testing altogether. Alter college admission requirements. Adjust grading scales. Abolish the honor roll, as New York City schools proposed before the 2021–2022 school year, because it is apparently "detrimental to students not making the grade."[3] To use our example from the last chapter, rather than encouraging Nemo to swim out of the filter tube, equity would demand that every fish in the tank get stuck in their own. As Rand says, it is "defiance of the Law of Causality: their demand for equal results from unequal causes—or equal rewards for unequal performance."[4]

Those pursuing equity never consider how those who lag behind might contribute to their own circumstances. They only ever focus on the erroneous assumption that those who are ahead have some kind of unfair advantage. Differences in cultural values and behaviors are never examined. Rather than working to change and improve these behaviors, the behaviors are deemed irrelevant or, if acknowledged, deemed to be the result of systemic bias. That means a child's inability to pay attention in class, stay in his seat, follow instructions, take notes, do his homework, and other issues that lead to poor test results are all evidence of systemic racism. This is one reason equity only equalizes downward: the lowest common denominator is the only real option. If we are not allowed to ask those who lag behind to improve themselves, then the only option is to lower everyone else down to their level.

Consider that some people are born with natural musical talent and are able to sing beautifully without much effort. Some have to work hard for years to sound decent. Some could sound decent if they spent time training, but they choose not to. Some are tone-deaf and can't stay on key to save their life. How would an equity initiative approach such an imbalance of outcomes? Shall we decide that no one is allowed to sing anymore? Should we change the definition and requirements of "good singing" so as to better accommodate tone-deaf singers? Should less-skilled singers be given contracts to record albums that the government then forces us to buy and listen to? Or should the people who are not great singers be encouraged to train and be provided with opportunities to do so? Or should they simply be encouraged to find something else at which they naturally excel and focus their efforts there?

This is the difference between racial equality and racial equity. Racial equality looks to remove race as a variable and strives to see that everyone is provided with an equal opportunity to fail or succeed by their own merit. Racial equity, on the other hand, seeks to ignore differences between individuals, make race the most important variable in the equation, and promote stereotypes and blatant racial discrimination in an attempt to manipulate outcomes. It is, again, an attempt to fight perceived, hidden racism with actual, open racism.

One of my favorite stories of open racism shrouded in claims of equity is when the Biden administration decided to institute a so-called "harm-reduction" grant program that would supposedly help drug addicts by funding "safe smoking kits/supplies." That means the Biden administration provided funding—in the form of dollars taken from taxpayers—for crack pipes and other drug paraphernalia, supposedly in order to help racial minorities. A federal program to fund street-drug smoking kits is pretty unbelievable on its own, but to say that it is explicitly to help non-white people is clearly outrageous—or at least it should be.

Such thinking is common within progressivism. The people who buy into the equity foolishness regularly suggest that non-white people need more help with things like using the internet and figuring out how to get an ID. In any other context, it would be considered wildly racist to say such things. Assuming someone listens to rap music because he is black would be considered a racist microaggression, but assuming he would benefit from a crack-pipe program or from abolishing photo ID requirements because he is black is apparently perfectly fine. Equity!

If People Are Equal, They Are Not Free

Apart from the open racism of racial equity, it is vital to understand that equality of outcomes is not an achievable goal, at least not in the sense that CRT advocates believe in. Because equity only equalizes downward, the only place people can ever truly be equal is at the bottom. That is not just speculation. History shows us how socialism and communism, in attempts to create societies where everyone is equal, have collapsed into ruin and despair. In countries like the former Soviet Union, Mao's China, Venezuela, Cuba, Cambodia, etc., attempts to establish equity have consistently ended in tyranny and atrocity. A quote often attributed to Aleksandr Solzhenitsyn says, "Human beings are born with different capacities. If they are free, they are not equal. If they are equal, they are not free."

In the Broadway musical *Anastasia* (based on the film of the same name), the character Dmitri makes a similar point about life in Communist Russia under Vladimir Lenin following the assassination of the Romanov family. In the first verse of the song, "A Rumor in St. Petersburg," he sings that "everyone is equal—professors push the brooms. Two dozen total strangers live in two small rooms."[5]

This song is a wonderful expression of the idea of equity. Equity in Soviet Russia meant everyone was equally impoverished and oppressed. I find it fascinating that Hollywood and Broadway, which are extremely left-leaning, accept this open rebuke of communism and the concept of equity without much resistance to speak of. Both Hollywood and

Broadway regularly push ideas of equity, but *Anastasia* is still popular in the theatrical community, and those in the theatre who promote the idea of equity seem not to recognize that this song directly criticizes them. Though, to be fair, it is not uncommon to see people fail to connect the dots between the horrific historical outcomes of socialism and communism and the idealistic fantasy that people support. They believe the failures in those other countries throughout history were due to something different than the ideals they embrace. "That wasn't real socialism" or "That wasn't real communism" are common retorts to any criticism. "Real communism has never been tried!" They believe those other people in those other societies just did it wrong. It will work this time!

The gap between what sounds good and what actually works has been the source of all manner of catastrophes throughout history. If we wish to correct disparities, we should focus on correcting the disparities between good intentions and disastrous results. This pursuit of racial equity is supposed to correct racial disparities with the assumption being, of course, that the disparities exist because there is some sort of systemic bias which can and should be corrected. We will explore that fallacy in the next chapter. But it isn't enough to simply say you want to correct racial disparities and then do whatever you want, ignoring the detrimental effects of your actions. Having the intention of helping is not the same as actually helping. It's like the scene from *Major Payne* when Payne "helps" a Marine who has been shot in the arm. In order to take his mind off the pain of his bullet wound, Payne takes the Marine's finger and gruesomely breaks it. "Ahh! My finger!" he screams, to which Payne responds, "Works every time."[6] Technically, it did momentarily take the Marine's mind off his arm, and it is a hilarious bit of comedy, but clearly this isn't an actual solution, no matter how well-intentioned.

More Liberty Means More Equality

There is a sense that we have the ability to make the world a better place simply by controlling other people's behavior. The assumption is that other people cannot be trusted to make the right decisions, so some centralized authority must do it for them. In other words, liberty must be sacrificed in the name of equity. Liberty is oppressive. Control is freedom. If only we can force people to adhere to a certain ideological perspective and do the things we want them to do, then utopia is at hand!

Nobel-Prize-winning economist Milton Friedman once said, "A society that puts equality—in the sense of equality of outcome—ahead of freedom will end up with neither equality nor freedom. . . . On the other hand, a society that puts freedom first will, as a happy byproduct, end up with greater freedom and greater equality."[7]

This is counterintuitive for a lot of people, particularly those who want power and who distrust liberty. When someone believes they have the power to manually shape society into their utopian vision, they also believe they are morally infallible and that they have such superior intellectual prowess that they should be allowed to compel others to bend the knee to their ideology. This always fails. To begin with, they are neither morally infallible nor intellectually superior. If they were, they would know that even if what they propose were ethical, the hundreds of millions of individuals in this country and their innumerable interactions cannot possibly be micromanaged by a centralized authority—at least not without doing so at the barrel of a gun and wiping out a large percentage of the population in the process. Every individual is different, every interaction is unique, and every motivation, intention, thought, idea, or word spoken exists on its own. The combinations of an infinite number of individual biological, cultural, and situational variables are never the same, and to believe you can somehow take hold of it all, implement your own subjective controls, and equalize those outcomes is unbelievably foolish and narcissistic at its core.

It is like the economic problems in Communist countries: central governments are unable to determine how much to produce of a given product and cannot efficiently manage resources. As a result, there are widespread shortages and people starve. There is a story about former Soviet Union President Mikhail Gorbachev asking British Prime Minister Margaret Thatcher how she saw to her people getting food—not realizing it was the free market that did that, not a centralized authority.

The idea of equality is the same. We could ask, "How do we see to it that our people get equality?" The answer is liberty. As long as rights are not being directly violated, people should be left alone to do what they think is best. What arises from these millions upon millions of unique individual behaviors and interactions is a massive, complex system that is far superior to anything some government or bureaucratic organization could ever even dream up, let alone implement.

CRT advocates fail to grasp that the inequality and oppression of the past was all facilitated by the government—a government that believed it should have the power to control and manipulate outcomes. Laws were passed, policies implemented, and government agents enforced controls that led to and perpetuated racial discrimination. This desire to control outcomes was what caused and perpetuated the race-based injustices throughout history. They fail to recognize that the market punished discrimination when allowed to operate freely; when the government did not or could not intervene, there was far more equality than otherwise. Economic incentives led businesses to hire more black workers, rent more apartments to black people, and desegregate public transportation; the central authority drove the segregation. It was the central authority that ensured that discrimination and segregation would persist. Such arguments are difficult for those who despise liberty and wish to control behavior they find abhorrent to swallow. The evidence, however, clearly shows that liberty is superior, and a free market does a much better job of regulating adverse behavior. Whatever central authority exists should only be responsible for protecting rights. Otherwise, the market will take care of itself.

The bottom line is that we should not be pursuing equity, regardless of what CRT advocates claim or how they try to appeal to emotion. Equal outcomes are impossible to achieve on any level, save equalizing everyone at the bottom. We should pursue equality before the law, we should pursue equal opportunity, and we should pursue the complete removal of race as a variable. That is only done by pursuing liberty. More liberty leads to more equality.

CHAPTER 9

Do Disparities Equal Bias?

When you truly believe that the racial groups are equal,
then you also believe that racial disparities must be the
result of racial discrimination.

—Ibram X. Kendi

One of the largest fallacies in Critical Race Theory—the fallacy that lies at its very core and gives rise to all others—is the assumption that differences in outcomes between racial groups automatically indicate racial bias. The presupposition here is that if there were no such thing as racial discrimination, then racial groups would always have the same outcomes. This claim is treated as a foregone, incontestable conclusion. But is it true?

That seems like an important question to consider before you begin tearing down institutions and instilling victim/oppressor ideology in young children. You should probably have some strong evidence that your basic premise is correct—and I don't mean evidence of the simple existence of disparities. I mean evidence that the results of such a univariate analysis are accurate and that the single causative variable of these disparities is, indeed, race. That is an extremely important question to answer, and the entirety of CRT ideology hinges on whether it is true. If the facts lead to another variable or set of variables outside of race, CRT immediately collapses.

So why does such an important, fundamental question just get glossed over? What kind of science ignores the fundamental question at the core of its own hypothesis to leap directly to a conclusion?

The answer to that question is "pseudoscience." *Merriam-Webster* defines pseudoscience as "a system of theories, assumptions, and methods erroneously regarded as scientific." Some warning signs of pseudoscience include ad hoc hypotheses employed to avoid having its claims proven false, a heavy reliance on jargon and anecdotes, and continually placing the burden of proof on those who push against it rather than on those making the claims. In other words, pseudoscientists use a lot of fancy words to make themselves seem legitimate and demand that you prove their claims wrong—which, by the way, can never really be proven wrong—while continually developing new ad hoc explanations for any evidence that might contradict them. A great example of this is flat-earth theory. I won't spend a lot of time on it here, but if you take a few moments to research it, you will immediately see flat-earthers have all sorts of ridiculous ways to explain away the plethora of evidence that the earth is round. For example, if you point to photos of Earth taken from space, they will say, "Well, those photos are fake." As such, their theory can never be proven false. It also means that any evidence you provide is dismissed and treated as further proof that their theory is correct. There is just some grand conspiracy to hide the real truth. Does that sound familiar?

In true millennial fashion, I'm going to use another *Harry Potter* reference to make my point. (Don't judge me.) But Luna Lovegood and her father, Xenophilius, are wonderful examples of the impenetrable power of pseudoscience. Throughout the books, they make claims that remain impervious both to the plethora of evidence against them and the lack of evidence supporting them. In *Harry Potter and the Order of the Phoenix*, Luna claims that the Minister of Magic has a private army of heliopaths (spirits of fire). When Hermione scoffs and asks for evidence, Luna calls her narrow-minded and says there are plenty of eyewitness accounts. Case closed.[1] In *The Deathly Hallows,* Hermione asks Xenophilius about a suspicious horn in his house. He responds that it came from a Crumple-Horned Snorkack, which does not exist in the world of *Harry Potter.* Hermione pushes back and informs him it is actually a highly dangerous, explosive magical object called an Erumpent horn and offers evidence for this from a book called *Fantastic Beasts and Where to Find Them.* Xenophilius, however, remains unswayed. He explains simply that he bought it from someone who knew of his interest in the Snorkack, as if that settles the matter. Hermione is right, of course, and the horn explodes at the end of the scene. But even that isn't enough to convince the Lovegoods. Later, when Luna is talking about the horn coming from a Snorkack, and Hermione reminds her that it exploded, proving that it was an Erumpent horn, Luna simply responds, "No, it was definitely a Snorkack horn. Daddy told me. It will probably have reformed by now. They mend themselves, you know."[2]

This is how it works. When it comes to Critical Race Theory, we are dealing with a bunch of Luna Lovegoods who continually make outrageous, unprovable claims, draw erroneous connections between two points, assume cause and effect without proof, rely on anecdotal evidence, and dismiss any evidence that contradicts them. With that said, they are far more insidious than Luna and her father, as they not only hold these beliefs, but demand that others be forced to adhere to them as well. It isn't enough for them to simply believe the horn came from a Crumple-Horned Snorkack and will not explode if touched, but you must publicly affirm their belief and also be forced to touch it to demonstrate your unwavering faith in the ideology. And if you refuse, you'll be canceled.

Let's take a moment to actually examine the central claim that "racial disparities indicate bias." Just on the surface, on a common sense level, it should already be clear that this is far too simplistic to have any real merit. Countless disparities exist between individuals and between groups regardless of race, gender, or any other immutable characteristic, so unless one believes that some sort of bias accounts for all these gaps, logic dictates there must be other underlying reasons at play. And if other variables account for disparities in these cases, then reasonably these variables cannot be discounted in disparities in other cases.

For example, consider poverty. Often, a CRT advocate will claim that black people remain in poverty because of racism. Such a claim ignores multiple things. For instance, it ignores the fact that the vast majority of black people do *not* live in poverty. It also ignores the millions of white people who do. The U.S. Census Bureau estimates the American population to be 331.8 million, with black Americans accounting for 13.6 percent of the population (approximately 45 million people) and white Americans accounting for 59.3 percent (approximately 196 million people).[3] The Census Bureau also reported that the poverty rate for white Americans in 2020 was 8.2 percent, or 16 million people. The poverty rate for black Americans in 2020 was 19.5 percent, or 8.7 million people.[4] What the CRT activist focuses on is the disparity in poverty *rates* (not actual numbers) and proclaims that this 19.5 percent figure is due to systemic racism. However, these numbers also indicate that not only do 16 million white people live in poverty, but 36 million black people (80.5 percent) do not!

How do you explain that? What variables contribute to those circumstances? If racism did not inhibit the black people who don't live in poverty, why does it inhibit those who do? If racism does not explain the millions of white people who live in poverty, then what does? And why wouldn't those things also explain black poverty? One might point to cultural issues known to perpetuate poverty regardless of race (e.g., poor education, an external locus of control, criminality, promiscuity, children born out of wedlock, absent fathers, etc.), but CRT advocates will give a Luna Lovegood-esque response along the lines of, "Racism creates and perpetuates the conditions that cause those behaviors." They sometimes will even acknowledge that disparities in outcomes are driven by disparities in behaviors and attitudes, but they will still blame it on racism anyway.

Cultural Hegemony and Structural Determinism

This is one of the primary difficulties of combating narratives around Critical Race Theory. Personal agency does not belong to the supposed victims; "the system" is responsible for everything, including individual behavior. The idea of cultural hegemony—a term coined by the Marxist Italian philosopher Antonio Gramsci—suggests that those in power create a system that oppresses the oppressed even without their knowledge by shaping the "values, norms, ideas, expectations, worldview, and behavior of the rest of society."[5] It essentially establishes a status quo and controls people's behavior through cultural and ideological domination. This idea, then, yields itself to structural determinism (a modification of the Marxian concept of "economic determinism"), which holds that the very structure of society and institutions predetermine outcomes for different groups. Determinism means that the things that happen and the choices made ultimately result from external factors as opposed to free will.

CRT advocates openly admit to embracing this idea of structural determinism, which is why they say ideas like institutional or systemic racism explain nearly everything. If it is true that our society is built on the foundation of white supremacy and that it shapes our "values, norms, ideas, expectations, worldview, and behavior," and it is also true that this white supremacist structure is deterministic and controls the outcomes of non-white groups, then it can only follow that non-white people have no real agency. They have no free will. Their behaviors are manipulated and controlled by the structure of society. They are completely beholden to this system of white supremacy even if they aren't consciously aware of it. Prevalent cultural and individual behavioral issues that are known to increase the probability of poor outcomes across all groups must be rejected and ignored. Instead, we must claim that these cultural and behavioral issues only exist because of systemic racism. It is a giant loop of circular reasoning.

An example of this kind of reasoning was seen in the case of Ma'Khia Bryant, a Columbus, Ohio, teenager who was shot and killed by a police officer in 2021 when she attacked another girl with a knife. Immediately, activists claimed the only reason the officer shot her was because she was black. However, the facts (and video) show some sort of fight was already underway when police arrived on the scene. Bryant, wielding a large knife, screamed at another girl, "I'm going to stab you!" (I am paraphrasing. Her actual language was much more colorful) as she swung the knife back in preparation to indeed stab the girl. The officer shot Bryant before she could do so.

Now, it should be noted that this case was extremely tragic. Any loss of life is terrible, but particularly this one because it involved a kid. But was it racism? If you review the footage, you will find that about nine seconds elapsed between the time the officer arrived on the scene, issued commands to drop the knife, and Bryant pulling it back to stab the other girl. Is it reasonable to believe that the officer's response to someone trying to stab someone else depended on race? Is it reasonable to believe that if Bryant were white, the officer would have allowed her to stab the other girl? It is worth noting that the girl who was about to get stabbed was also black. Why wouldn't the perspective be that the officer actually saved a black life? If shooting Bryant was truly a racist act, why was she the only one shot even though there were multiple black people on the scene? The logic completely crumbles with even the slightest bit of analysis.

These seem like reasonable questions to ask, but those who embraced the racist narrative nonetheless remained unswayed. They determined that Bryant was a victim of systemic racism, a victim of structural determinism. The system caused the circumstances which led to the behavior that caused her death. We are supposed to believe that if it weren't for systemic racism, she never would have been in that situation in the first place. These kinds of reasoning tactics ensure that the theory of systemic racism can never be proven false. Everything that happens serves as evidence to support the theory—even evidence that directly contradicts it. Yes, yes, the horn exploded. But that's obviously just more evidence that it came from the Snorkack.

We saw this in the Jussie Smollett case as well. Race activists' initial reactions were almost gleeful. "Finally! An example of tangible racism that can be exploited to help prop up our outrageous claims! Hooray!" Media outlets were all over it, lamenting the horrendous state of our racist country. Race hustlers were delivering speeches and linking arms together like they were at some kind of civil rights cosplay convention. Black opportunists were crying alligator tears on TV and talking about how terrifying it is to be black in twenty-first-century Jim Crow America. Celebrities were throwing their fists up and proclaiming solidarity with the black people they claimed couldn't even go outside without being attacked with bleach and a noose.

Unfortunately for all of them, the entire narrative turned out to be a giant farce. Every single bit of it was a lie. How did the activists respond? By shrugging it off and saying that at least Smollett had started a conversation that is necessary because these things happen every day.

Are you kidding me? To them, the hoax wasn't actually a hoax. It was an important spotlight needed to expose the real problems of systemic racism in our country. Smollett was simply responding to that need. His actions were a product of the structure of the system!

There is no proving arguments like this wrong. Being wrong just means the people making these arguments were even more right than they initially believed they were. The wrongness indicates how far we still have to go as a country to accept their rightness. Don't ask them to explain this. They aren't here to educate you. Do the work!

Police Shootings

One of the most potent weapons of emotional manipulation wielded by those who peddle victimhood is the racial disparities that exist within the criminal justice system, particularly when it comes to police shootings. The first thing to recognize is that the rhetoric around them is extremely hyperbolic and full of misinformation. That is almost entirely the media's fault. Many people believe that unarmed black people are constantly being gunned down by racist cops because that is the narrative the mainstream media promotes. In early 2021, the Skeptic Research Center released a survey examining how informed people were about race and policing. The results showed that 84 percent of people who identified as "very liberal" believed police killed more than 100 unarmed black people in 2019. Fifty-three percent believed it was more than 1,000. Twenty-two percent believed the number was 10,000 or more. Among those who identified as "liberal," 78 percent believed it was 100 or more, 39 percent believed it was 1,000 or more, and 12 percent believed it was 10,000 or more.[6]

The actual number of unarmed black people killed by police in 2019 was twelve.[7]

How can we even begin to discuss the relationship between disparities and bias if people don't have even a minimal grasp of the facts of the given situation? Of course it's going to seem like bias is driving police shootings if you believe that more than ten thousand people of a certain race are killed compared to zero of another race. In my own research, I have found that not only do people heavily overestimate the number of unarmed black people who are killed by police, but they grossly underestimate the number of unarmed white people who are. Many think it never happens. The truth is that in 2019, police killed twenty-six unarmed white people. How is this possible? More than twice as many unarmed white people were killed that year than unarmed black people, and yet people believed that far more black people were killed—even multiple thousands more.

This is always shocking to people who buy into media narratives. What generally happens next is an uncomfortable scrambling as they contend with their cognitive dissonance; they eventually fall on something called "disparate impact." This is, again, a way of throwing in new explanations to combat evidence against one's theory in order to keep it from being proven false. So those duped by the media will then claim that even though more white people are killed by police, black people are killed at a higher rate per capita. They'll say black people comprise only 13 percent of the population and account for 25 percent of police shootings. Two hundred fifty-one black people were killed by police in 2019 (that's a rate of five per million). Four hundred twenty-four white people were killed by police that year, so that's a rate of two per million.[8] That means black people were 2.5 times more likely to be killed by police. Aha! Bias!

Once again, if race is the only variable you think is pertinent, these kinds of arguments may seem compelling. But there are clearly other variables at play. Does it make sense to compare police shootings between two groups without also comparing crime rates? Does it make sense to ignore the circumstances of the shootings? As we already mentioned, police killed only twelve unarmed black people in 2019 out of the 251 total. That means that 239, or 95 percent, of the black suspects killed were armed. Consider also that 398, or 94 percent, of the 424 white people killed were armed. So, as a percentage of those killed by police, white suspects were actually more likely to be killed while unarmed. Systemic racism!

Now let's examine the violent crime rates for 2019 for each group:

Murder:
White–2 per 100,000
Black–11 per 100,000

Rape:
White–6 per 100,000
Black–10 per 100,000

Robbery:
White–12 per 100,000
Black–67 per 100,000

Aggravated Assault:
White–85 per 100,000
Black–207 per 100,000

Weapons:
White–30 per 100,000
Black–103 per 100,000

As you can see, the crime rates for black people were several times higher in every violent crime category except rape, which is only 1.5 times higher.[9] When a group has a much higher rate of violent crime—one whose murder rate alone is five times higher than another group—is it unreasonable to expect that police will kill them at a higher rate?

What would happen if you leveled out the violent crime rates?

Consider that white suspects committed 209,848 violent crimes in 2019 and black suspects committed 129,346.[10] If you look only at these numbers and compare them to police shootings, you see that police killed twenty white suspects for every 10,000 white people arrested for violent crime, and nineteen black suspects for every 10,000 arrests for violent crime. How is this possible?! The data, again, suggest that police are more likely to kill white suspects. Also, the fact that the overall disparity completely vanishes and even reverses when zooming in on violent crime suggests that the disparities we see when looking at the overall population are driven by the large differences in violent crime rates (not by racial bias). As author Heather Mac Donald often points out, not only are the disparities explained by crime rates, but the data show that black people are actually killed less often than the crime rates would predict.[11]

In truth, of course, races do not commit crimes. Individuals do. Races are not killed by police. Individuals are. These situations nearly always involve individuals engaged in antisocial behavior who are reaping the consequences of that behavior. Activists like to focus on the exceptions where police make a mistake, or when someone is killed under questionable circumstances. But the fact is that police rarely kill anybody of any race. Each year, about 1,000 suspects total are killed by police[12] out of around ten million arrests.[13] That's 0.0003 percent of the U.S. population and 0.01 percent of all arrests. That number doesn't include all the contacts police have with people that don't end in arrest. If it is rare for police to kill any suspects of any race for any reason, then logically, it is even rarer for them to kill someone who is unarmed; even rarer than that for police to kill someone who is unarmed under questionable circumstances; and even rarer than *that* for police to kill someone who is unarmed under questionable circumstances who is black. It would be foolish to believe such a thing is commonplace. The racist killer cop narrative is a farce.

Predictably, these facts are wholly irrelevant to those who wish to cling to the narratives of racial bias and victimhood. The shooting disparities take priority as evidence of racism. The disparities in crime rates, if they are even acknowledged, are once again attributed to systemic racism. Professional victims blame them either on false reports (which means one would have to assume that the majority of the black people accused of committing these crimes are actually innocent) or the environment and the system, which they claim is a product of racism and white supremacy. It is exhausting. Of course, this isn't to say there is never any racism or bias. But it is to say that in the grand scheme of things, these disparities are not driven by some kind of systemic oppression. Police are clearly not hunting down and killing black people for the crime of being black.

When contending with such flawed logic, one must ask why it does not carry over into other group disparities. What if we examined 2019 police shootings by gender? Men accounted for 72 percent of suspects arrested[14] and a whopping 96 percent of those killed by police.[15] Is that evidence of misandry? Or are there other variables to consider, like differences in violent crime rates and circumstances around the arrest? If variables like these are enough to explain such substantial disparities between men and women, then why wouldn't they also explain much smaller disparities between racial groups?

Destructive Progressive Policies

The truth of all of this makes it especially egregious that parents are teaching their children to be afraid of police officers and lamenting that their children risk being gunned down by law enforcement if they leave the house. Meanwhile, children are being slaughtered in the streets every day by black gang members who have no regard for human life. In a bit of cruel irony, the measures that activists claim promote racial equity end up providing leniency to dangerous criminals through bail and sentencing policies, allowing them to return to the streets to further terrorize neighborhoods and murder black people. There is something really twisted about expressing fear over police murdering black children while protecting criminals who actually do murder black children.

Consider these stories:

- In January 2022, a six-month-old boy in Atlanta, Georgia, named Grayson Fleming-Gray was shot and killed when the car he was riding in with his mother was hit by gunfire. The shooter was a man named Dequasie Little, who, according to Fox Atlanta, had a criminal history that spanned "four and a half years, four counties, six arrests, seven victims, and now a murder charge."[16]
- In February 2022, an eleven-year-old in Houston, Texas, named D. J. Dugas was shot and killed by a man named Daveyonne Howard. Howard was breaking into cars when the owner caught him in the act. Howard pulled a gun and began shooting; one of the bullets hit D. J., who was getting a coat out of a nearby car. Howard also had an extensive criminal history but was out on bail for aggravated robbery at the time of D. J.'s death.[17]
- In May 2022, a one-year-old in Pittsburgh, Pennsylvania, named De'Avry Thomas was killed in a drive-by shooting. His killers, Londell Falconer and Markez Anger, both had extensive histories of felony charges, and both were out on nonmonetary bail at the time of the shooting.[18]

These are only three examples of many in which young children, more often than not young black children, are gunned down in their neighborhoods while playing outside, asleep in their beds, riding in a car with their parents, playing video games in their homes—just trying to be kids and live their lives. At least seventy-one children under the age of thirteen were murdered in street violence in 2021,[19] and at least seventy-eight in 2020.[20] That's at least 149 young children gunned down in two years. And more often than not, the person who gunned them down was also black and almost certainly had a long history of criminality as well as a history of leniency from the so-called white supremacist criminal justice system.

Oftentimes we hear that black communities are over-policed and black people are unfairly and disproportionately targeted, arrested, charged, and sentenced. This, professional victims claim, is incontrovertible evidence of systemic racism. But is it? Is any of that true? If it is, then how is it possible that so many people roam the streets with rap sheets longer than *War and Peace*, wreaking havoc on innocent people only to be arrested, shoved back into the system, and promptly spit right back out to do it all again? Why do police have such a difficult time solving murders committed by black people? Chicago, for example, had a murder clearance rate of 44.5 percent in 2020, and the vast majority of the unsolved murders were gang-related.[21] If police were targeting significant numbers of innocent black people, why would the murder clearance rate be so low? You will recall from the FBI Uniform Crime Report that black perpetrators commit over 50 percent of all murders in the U.S., and that's even with a significant number of suspects getting away with it.

In order to accept that the systemic racism claim exists, we need to contend with the logic around it. Given the facts we just discussed— if, indeed, "the system" is unfairly targeting, arresting, charging, and convicting black people—then that must mean innocent black people are being railroaded in large numbers while guilty black people go free. Think about it. We know, for a fact, that a significant number of murders and other crimes are committed by people with long criminal histories, and yet, they remain free. We also know for a fact that a significant number of people are committing murders and getting away with it as the cases go unsolved (more than half of them in Chicago alone), and people with knowledge of what happened refuse to help police. So we must assume this systemically racist system cares more about punishing innocent black people than it does about punishing guilty black people. Does that make sense? Is that evidence of a racially biased system, or is something else going on?

Correlation Is Not Causation

Also consider that one of the primary arguments on this topic involves the number of black people in prison, which is assumed to be tied to the war on drugs. Race activists claim that high incarceration rates of black people stem from police unfairly arresting them for low-level drug crimes, like possession of marijuana. However, if you look at the Bureau of Justice Statistics, which issues reports on prison populations, at the end of 2019, only 2.8 percent of black state penitentiary inmates' worst crime was drug possession.[22] By comparison, 64 percent were in for violent crime and 12 percent were in for property crime. Does that seem like drugs are driving incarceration? Even if you add in the more serious charge of drug trafficking, the incarceration rate is still only 12 percent. The vast majority of black people in prison are there because of violent crime, not drugs. It is also worth noting that 5.3 percent of white inmates were in for drug possession and 16.6 percent if you include trafficking. Systemic racism?

Another common claim is that white and black people have disparate sentencing rates for similar crimes. What most often happens is someone will compare a cherrypicked case of a white person receiving a relatively lenient sentence to one of a black person receiving a harsher sentence, then claim that the different outcomes demonstrate systemic racism. This practice ignores all the cases of white people who received harsher sentences than black people. It also ignores cases in which white people received harsher sentences than other white people and black people received more lenient sentences than other black people. If you cherrypick your samples, you are guaranteed to find some that fit your preconceived notions.

But the problem with such comparisons is that they only examine a few surface-level details. The people making them do not consider the facts of different defendants with different criminal histories, in different places (often different states), under different crime circumstances, making different pleas, facing different courtroom attitudes, or that they are represented by different lawyers competing against different prosecutors under the watch of different judges, etc. The list of differences is innumerable. If one could control for all those variables, maybe we could expect identical outcomes. If a single judge is caught handing down disparate sentencing, then he/she should have to answer for that. But comparing completely different situations that involve completely different people makes very little sense. That isn't to say the criminal justice system is perfect—far from it. But claims of racism need to carry extensive evidence, not flimsy accusations.

Disparities exist everywhere and do not automatically indicate bias. We already discussed the disparities between men and women. There are also massive disparities between the young and the elderly. Younger people are disproportionately targeted, arrested, sentenced, and killed by police compared to elderly people, and their neighborhoods draw a much heavier police presence than retirement communities. Is that an equity issue? Is it systemic ageism? What about the disproportionate number of people with athletic builds who are in great shape who get to compete in Olympic gymnastics? Why can't out-of-shape, overweight people who can't do any kind of flips at all be brought on the Olympic team to compete in the balance beam? Such disparities surely indicate institutional ableism. According to the U.S. Centers for Disease Control and Prevention, black children are seven times more likely to drown than white children.[23] Does that mean water is racist? Do white supremacists construct pools? Do floaties only work for white children?

These are silly examples, but they illustrate the point. How about we consider a more serious example, like the fact that Asian-Americans, along with multiple immigrant groups including Indian-Americans and Nigerian-Americans, out-earn white Americans every year? Is that systemic racism? Is the system biased against white people and in favor of these other groups? Shouldn't we launch an equity initiative to ensure that white people earn as much as Asian-Americans? It is quite a system of white supremacy when not only must racism operate invisibly and secretly, but white people aren't even at the top of it!

Consider also the issue of absent fathers and its effects. According to the National Fatherhood Initiative, children who grow up without fathers in the home are significantly more likely to end up in poverty, suffer from behavioral problems, commit crimes, end up in prison, experience teen pregnancy, abuse drugs and alcohol, suffer from obesity, drop out of school, or commit suicide.[24] With that in mind, what do you think the predictable result would be if a certain demographic had a higher rate of absent fathers than another group? Are we supposed to believe that the fact that 71 percent of black children being born out of wedlock compared to 29 percent of white children has no effect on outcomes?[25] I suppose race activists would say this, too, is due to structural determinism and suggest that this substantial disparity of children born out of wedlock is, itself, driven by systemic racism. Their parents have no agency, according to the Critical Race theorists.

This is the bottom line: Critical Race Theory would have us believe that racial disparities are evidence of racial bias, regardless of what the evidence actually says. It would have us believe that correlation equals causation. But neither speculation and assumptions, nor pseudoscience and dogmatic ideology, nor mere differences between group outcomes are a legitimate basis for accusing someone of racism. Disparities do not equal bias.

CHAPTER 10

The Demand for Racism

The most striking irony of the age of white guilt is that racism suddenly became valuable to the people who had suffered it.

—Shelby Steele

I am not sure who coined the phrase, but it has been said that in America, "the demand for racism exceeds the supply." It is a pithy phrase that carries a tremendous amount of truth. Our society is utterly race-obsessed, but there is not nearly enough actual racism to justify this obsession. There is a sort of romanticization of historical events like slavery and the civil rights movement, so much so that both pieces of history are constantly dragged into the present by people pretending that the events that occurred back then are still happening. Many professional victims view themselves as something like reincarnated abolitionists and civil rights leaders, donning the costumes of these historical figures and waving the flags of oppression and revolution. Anything perceived as a racial issue is given far more weight than anything else. The word "nigger" coming from the lips of a white person has the power to bring the entire country to its knees, conjuring up an exponentially deeper and more visceral emotional reaction than that of hundreds of brown-skinned children being gunned down in street violence.

Think about that for a moment. A nasty word aimed at a black person (or even innocuously uttered while singing along with a rap song) is considered to be far more offensive than a black child being murdered in a drive-by shooting. How does that make any sense?

Additionally, the race-obsessed continually insist that racism is generally rampant and pervasive, that black people remain oppressed and marginalized, that white people—particularly white conservatives—are the same as those who harassed, tormented, and lynched black people in the past. This all serves to perpetuate perceptions of victimhood and to induce a feeling that we are somehow forever trapped in the racial climate of the 1800s.

The problem with these claims, apart from the obvious psychological issues of living in the past, is that they simply lack evidence. One only needs to look around to see we do not live in anything that even remotely resembles the 1800s and that black people are not being systematically oppressed. It just isn't true. You can certainly try to convince yourself otherwise, but the real-life evidence refutes you at every turn. It is difficult to maintain the illusion of pervasive racial oppression when America twice elects a black president, black people dominate the entertainment and sports industries, have their hands all over academia, continually show up in high-level positions throughout all industries, and when corporations bow down to every black-related cause. So we must ask: how does one convince others that they are indeed victims, that racism is a massive problem in our society, and that it is dangerous for them to live in America as a racial minority without any direct evidence to support these claims?

Racism Hoaxes

One way to accomplish this is to just completely fabricate it. Remember our discussion on St. George the Dragon Slayer? If there are no dragons available, you must create them! One must ask himself why, if there is truly a pervasive dragon problem and there are dragons everywhere you look, and you cannot possibly move without running into a dragon (or at least a micro-dragon), anyone would feel the need to create a fake one. In order to get people to recognize that dragons are rampaging through your neighborhood, you prop up a giant stuffed dragon and proclaim the fearsome beast is attacking you. Why would you do that if there are plenty of real dragons terrorizing you? In the same way, if racism is truly endemic and black people are truly oppressed, why would race hoaxes be so prevalent? Why would anyone need to fabricate attacks? There should be plenty of examples of real racial oppression to draw from.

We have already discussed the bizarre case of Jussie Smollett. But he is far from the only one who has weaponized race in an attempt to benefit from the lie of racial oppression. There are endless examples of people claiming to be the target of racial harassment and violence only to be exposed as liars; examples of people faking racist graffiti only to be exposed as the ones who made it; and examples of people simply attributing something negative to a "white supremacist" only to find out that the perpetrator was actually black. Over and over again, we are bombarded with stories of overt racism that conjure up widespread outrage and calls for justice, but then we discover that none of it was true. It is too late by that time, of course. Far more people hear the lie than the retraction.

For instance, when the media pushed the hoax that President Trump called white supremacists "very fine people," the story went everywhere. It dominated the news cycle. The anger all over the nation was palpable. There were all sorts of think pieces about the implications of having a president and an administration that supports white supremacists. It was a running theme in the media's attacks against Trump during his entire presidency. The only problem was that it wasn't true. But when the retraction was published and the lie was acknowledged, very few people saw it or heard about it. To this day, few people are aware that the initial story was a lie.

Such behavior has become commonplace in our society. Many people don't realize just how often these hoaxes happen. Let us consider a few other recent examples:

- For much of 2021, a neighborhood in Douglasville, Georgia, was terrorized by racist messages left in mailboxes supposedly by a member of the Ku Klux Klan. The messages included threats to burn down black people's homes and even kill them. This generated a lot of outrage and fear in the community. By October of that year, the police had figured out who was sending the messages and arrested the culprit: Terresha Lucas, a black woman.[1]

- In April 2021, a student at Viterbo University in La Crosse, Wisconsin, named Victoria Unanka claimed that she was the victim of multiple racist incidents and that someone set her dorm on fire in an apparent hate crime. There was outrage on campus and throughout the community. Surveillance video later proved that Unanka set the fire herself. Viterbo's president sent out a statement after the arrest but did not mention Unanka's race or the fact that it was a hoax.[2]

- Also in April 2021, someone sent out a series of racist messages and death threats on social media to black students at White Bear Lake High School in White Bear Lake, Minnesota. A white student was accused of running the account and sending out the messages. Students staged a walkout in protest, demanding justice. However, investigators discovered that a black student was actually behind the account. In response to this revelation, the superintendent issued a statement claiming the student was merely trying to draw attention to racial injustice.[3]

- In August 2021, racist graffiti and swastikas were discovered at Emory University in Atlanta, Georgia. The school sent a message to staff members saying how painful it was, that the university would be there for support, and pointing out the need for healing. After investigating, the police arrested Roy Lee Gordon, a black man and former employee. When the university updated the faculty and students on his arrest, administrators did not mention his race.[4]

- In February 2022, a student at Southern Illinois University named Kaliyeha Clark-Mabins reported to police that she had received hateful and threatening messages, including notes telling her to die and saying that black people didn't belong at the school. Two white students were accused of sending the messages. This prompted race activists to start a Change.org petition and to protest on campus, calling for the expulsion of the white students. Eventually, investigators discovered that Clark-Mabins wrote the letters to herself. The activists disappeared and the Change.org petition was closed.[5]

- In March 2022, racist graffiti was discovered at McClatchey High School in Sacramento, California. Someone had written "Colored" and "White" over water fountains in the school. The community was outraged. Parents and race activists came to the school to protest and demand that the racist students be held accountable. The school later discovered that the culprit was a black student.[6]

These are only a handful of incidents in a long list of racism hoaxes. A couple of good sources, if you are interested, are Wilfred Reilly's book *Hate Crime Hoax*[7] as well as the database at Fakehatecrimes.org, which has chronicled more than four hundred such incidents.[8] These hoaxes all follow the same theme: hate-crime claim is made, claim is accepted without any scrutiny or skepticism, outrage ensues, incident is treated as extremely significant and indicative of a systemically racist country, investigation later reveals the hoax, story is downplayed and vanishes.

This, again, isn't to say that racism does not exist. Of course it does. It just isn't exclusive to white people. Racism exists among all people groups. As long as there is evil and darkness in the world, man will continue to find arbitrary reasons to hate his fellow man. Even if we somehow manage to wipe racism off the face of the earth tomorrow, there will be people who will begin to hate each other for the shape of their earlobes. That shadow of human nature can never be eliminated this side of Heaven. But by crying wolf and falsifying that darkness, you diminish the real thing, disrespect its real victims, and make it difficult for any thinking person to believe any future claims.

The word "racism" has been so watered down in recent years that it has lost much of its potency. The endless onslaught of racism claims has done absolutely nothing to eliminate actual racism and, in fact, has instead worsened the problems of racial tension and division. By demanding that everyone hyperfocus on race or by expanding the net to include everything that bothers you or everything you disagree with under the umbrella of racism, you diminish the meaning of the word and inherently drive enmity. Embracing the idea that racism is invisible and subconscious, and that white people engage in racist acts and benefit from racism without even being aware of it, inherently drives enmity. Faking racist acts to make racism seem like a larger problem than it is inherently drives enmity.

Critical Race Theory gives us insight into the root of these hoaxes and the motives behind them, but they are not restricted to race. There are many other examples of fake hate crimes involving groups like LGBT people and Muslims. What they all share is a desire and intention to be seen as a victim. If a woman sees herself as an abused spouse and wants others to view her that way, but her husband doesn't actually abuse her, what might she do? How does one resolve such an identity crisis? It seems that fabricating victimization is the answer. The people fabricating hate-crime hoaxes weren't being treated like the victims that they believed they were, and they had to fix that. The girl who set her dorm on fire said, "No one was listening to me anymore." She was upset that others were not taking her victimhood claims seriously enough. She needed tangible proof.

Racial Hypersensitivity

Another way professional victims resolve this demand for racism is to seek out elements of popular culture that can be exploited and proclaim them to be racially problematic. A certain book, film, or TV series may land in the crosshairs of racial activists for not having enough black or brown characters, casting actors in a certain way, not adhering to historical accuracy, or whatever perceived offense they can conjure up in the moment. Cancel mobs will attack actors, musicians, and athletes, claiming something they said was racist. Products in stores and the companies that make them will be lambasted if anything about them can be perceived as racially insensitive.

For example, the film *Dune*, based on the book series by Frank Herbert, was denounced for its "white savior" themes.[9] The Netflix series *Cobra Kai* has been criticized for being "too white."[10] New York Yankees third baseman Josh Donaldson was called a racist and suspended for referring to Tim Anderson, a black player, as "Jackie" (even though Anderson had referred to himself as "the next Jackie Robinson").[11] Jon Gruden, head coach of the NFL's Las Vegas Raiders, was forced to resign after it was revealed that he had mocked the lip size of a man who happened to be black.[12] The logo and name of Aunt Jemima's syrup were changed for allegedly using a racist stereotype,[13] as were those of Uncle Ben's rice.[14]

The media stories about how some innocuous thing actually carries a history of racism and white supremacy or drives racial inequity are seemingly endless. There is a running joke that you can google the question "Is _ racist?", insert any word you can think of into the blank, and find articles on the subject. *Is cereal racist? Is sleep racist? Is Google racist?* All of these searches will yield results of people claiming each of these things are, indeed, racist and problematic. Try it yourself.

The *Washington Post* ran an article in June 2021 under the headline, "The Racist Legacy Many Birds Carry: Birders Grapple with Complicated Past Linked to Slavery, White Supremacy."[15] What could possibly be the purpose of such an article? How ridiculous has our society become that we feel we need to grapple with the supposed racism in birdwatching? Such nonsense would appear to be satire if you didn't know better. It is appalling that this is a serious piece put forth by one of the nation's most prestigious newspapers.

What is the result of such hypersensitivity? Who is truly helped? How does the world improve? What did taking Aunt Jemima's picture off a syrup bottle accomplish? In what way did suspending Tim Anderson improve race relations in professional baseball? Who was actually injured by watching *Dune*? How does life get better by announcing that cereal, sleep, search engines, and even birdwatching are racist? It's all ridiculous.

Beyond that, it is clear that these antics are fraudulent. If race activists truly believed what they are saying and a history of racism or an association with a racist past is something that needs to be addressed and dismantled to make the world better, they would not ignore the extremely racist history of the Democratic Party, which is directly responsible for perpetuating slavery, for Jim Crow, and for the resurgence of the Ku Klux Klan. How can this be ignored? Oftentimes, they will deflect those facts by saying, "But the parties switched!" to insinuate that the verifiable sins of the Democratic Party have been actively committed by Republicans since sometime in the 1960s, which isn't remotely true. No one can deny that the Democratic Party did all those things. The history of the Democrats is far more insidious than Aunt Jemima or birdwatching. Yet we are supposed to ignore it.

Another example is the glossed-over history of Planned Parenthood and founder Margaret Sanger's views on racial eugenics. Sanger initiated the Negro Project, which aimed to control the black population (and undesirable populations in general) through birth control. She gave a speech to a women's auxiliary meeting of the Ku Klux Klan. She told the *New York Times* that

> Birth control is not contraception indiscriminately and thoughtlessly practiced. It means the release and cultivation of the better racial elements in our society and the gradual suppression, elimination and eventual extinction of defective stocks—those human weeds which threaten the blooming of the finest flowers of American civilization.[16]

Sanger also wrote in a letter to Procter & Gamble soap company heir and fellow eugenicist Clarence Gamble,

We do not want word to go out that we want to extermi-
nate the Negro population, and the minister is the man
who can straighten out that idea if it ever occurs to any of
their more rebellious members.[17]

In April 2021, Planned Parenthood President April McGill Johnson did publicly address Sanger's history of racism and support of
eugenics in a *New York Times* op-ed, though she backed off on a
hardline accusation of racism and did not mention Gamble or the
Negro Project. Nonetheless, she also said, "Sanger remains an influential part of [Planned Parenthood's] history and will not be erased."[18]
Instead, she said Planned Parenthood would commit to fight supposed
systemic racism and establish "new diversity, equity, and inclusion
standards for affiliates seeking to be a part of the Planned Parenthood
Federation."

It is commendable that Johnson at least acknowledges her organization's abhorrent history, even if she follows by virtue-signaling a
commitment to DEI and antiracism. But the question becomes: How
can someone who believes in the tenets of Critical Race Theory, which
Johnson clearly does, also believe that an organization founded by a
person who embraced racial eugenics can and should continue to
operate? Why does the fact that black women have abortions over
four times more often than white women at Planned Parenthood
facilities—which intentionally target black women through both
marketing and location—not trigger the antiracism alarms?[19] Planned
Parenthood's own website promotes "reproductive justice" for black
women,[20] "black organizing" which claims to take action regarding
"sexual liberation, healing, and combating oppressive systems,"[21]
antiracism resources,[22] race equity toolkits,[23] support for Black Lives
Matter,[24] etc., and yet, no race activists complain about these targeted
campaigns or the resulting "disproportionate impact."

If we are to believe in CRT's presuppositions, we must assume white supremacy has wholly infected the system and that such disparate treatment and outcomes are due to racism. We are supposed to embrace nuance and extend grace to Planned Parenthood—nuance and grace that seem to be only reserved for progressive causes and organizations. But if talk show host Megyn Kelly must be fired simply for asking if wearing blackface while dressing up for Halloween as a kid is okay,[25] surely Planned Parenthood must be permanently shut down for its historical racial sins and current racial disparities.

There is no real logic or reason here. Actual solutions and positive outcomes seem to be a low priority for race activists. All that seems to matter is generating faux outrage, collecting virtue points, and validating one's own sense of victimhood or saviorism. As we discussed in Chapter 5, there appears to be no incentive to eliminate racial grievance. There is, however, a large incentive to perpetuate it, especially for those who have built their careers around it and for those who seek to use it to gain power and influence.

Victimhood and Power

One thing I find telling about this culture of victimhood and the essence of CRT in general is that real victims usually don't want to be viewed as victims. People who have been legitimately victimized don't often seek out the spotlight to put their victimhood on display. They don't usually seek to capitalize on their victimhood, and they certainly don't seek to be identified by it. A great example of this is the Jacob Blake shooting. A police officer in Kenosha, Wisconsin, shot Blake after he wrestled with cops, fought off a taser, refused to drop a knife, and tried to get into a vehicle containing a child. Blake was already wanted for sexual assault; the police were summoned to the scene where Blake was ultimately shot because he was violating a restraining order his victim had sought. After the incident, Blake and every black person who empathized with him were seen as the victims. The woman who called the police on Blake, whom he had sexually assaulted, was not. Blake lifted himself up as a victim. She did not. Even though she was the only true victim in the situation, she did not pursue and was not granted victim status.

True victims of trauma generally are not quick to advertise their experience to garner sympathy. This isn't always the case, of course, but it is very rarely a source of pride. When people market their victimhood and use supposed trauma as a political weapon, the motives are suspect. The leaders of the civil rights movement did not focus on victimhood, but on strength and unity. Those who participated did not want to be seen as victims. Even after the Civil War, the newly freed slaves did not want to be viewed as victims. It is quite phenomenal that black people in the twenty-first century feel and act more oppressed and victimized than those who directly experienced slavery. How is such a thing possible?

Shelby Steele, a fellow at the Hoover Institution and author of *White Guilt*, has hypothesized that the reason racial grievance continues to be weaponized is because black power and white guilt are the same thing.[26] He meant that black activists figured out that they were able to harness the shame and injustice of the past, create a sense of collective culpability for that shame and injustice among certain white people, and use their debilitating fear of being labeled a racist to manipulate, influence, and gain power for themselves. By seizing on a perceived lack of moral authority around race, black people are able to dominate conversations and shape race-based policy. White people, without moral authority on issues of race, are not permitted to object. If you listen to race activists speak, they will admit this explicitly. They will say that white people must be quiet and vacate spaces to make room for black voices. It is not based on the merit of ideas or the quality of the voice, but on the race of the person it belongs to. Out of fear and guilt, white people often capitulate.

If we revisit the core philosophy of Critical Race Theory, i.e., the idea that racism is endemic and infused in our institutions, it becomes clear why such an ideology might be attractive to so many people. Steele's theory on white guilt and black power would suggest that an ideology like Critical Race Theory allows white people who adhere to it to claim moral authority and virtue points they would not otherwise have while allowing black people to garner sympathy and gain power.

This explains why the demand for racism would be so high, despite its lack of actual supply. It would make sense for claims of oppression and victimization to be so pervasive and more prevalent now than during periods when real oppression was far more commonplace. It would make sense that collective guilt and collective victimhood would be primary weapons and why racial unity would not be a priority.

If white guilt equals black power, then your path to power as a black activist is hindered only by the level of guilt you can induce in white people. Victimhood becomes a currency. It becomes a way to increase one's status. It becomes a way to establish and maintain a career. It becomes a way to manipulate and coerce others in order to control behavior and shape public policy. It becomes a way to validate one's own identity. Victimhood becomes power itself.

CHAPTER 11

Up from Slavery

I have begun everything with the idea that I could
succeed, and I never had much patience with the
multitudes of people who are always ready to explain
why one cannot succeed.

—Booker T. Washington

I t is not possible to have a discussion on Critical Race Theory, or race
in general, without discussing slavery. At its core, Critical Race
Theory promotes the belief that historical injustices have so deeply
affected our society that they continue to significantly impact
present-day outcomes. Those who worship at the altar of race politics
consider American slavery and the racism underlying it to be our
original sin—a sin for which there is no actual redemption. The prevailing notion is that slavery has uniquely impacted black Americans
and can explain the racial disparities that exist today, particularly in
wealth and education.

There is no denying that history has some impact on the
present. Denying that would be foolish. However, to claim that
your current difficulties in life are a result of something that happened more than 150 years ago is a hard sell, especially in a country
like the United States. It might be somewhat different in a country
where you are born into a certain class and doomed to remain there
for the entirety of your life. But in America, class and income

mobility are the rule, not the exception. Most people move fluidly between income classes throughout their lives. The rich do not remain rich, and the poor do not remain poor. Less than 1 percent of the American population remain in the bottom 20 percent of wage earners over the course of their lives.[1] Birth is not destiny. That is the beauty of the American dream.

Claiming that something that happened before you were born is responsible for your life circumstances as an adult is difficult to swallow. If we remove ourselves from the racial context and imagine something terrible happening to our grandparents long before we were ever thought of, would it be sensible to claim that our current life situation is a direct result of what happened to them? It seems silly to even suggest it. Some people might say yes, but I find that claim outrageous. There are infinite variables to consider between the event in question and your current situation. Your grandparents and parents made countless choices, as did you, that led to the moment in which you currently find yourself. Think about all the decisions you have made throughout your life, and how they have impacted your circumstances to place you on the path where you currently stand. To blame your decisions and their subsequent consequences on your grandparents, let alone ancestors you have never known, is asinine. Your own choices and behavior have far more impact on your outcomes than something that happened before you were even born. How can we possibly claim that things we never experienced ourselves are the reason for our own life situations? How can we lay claim to the suffering of others? How can we claim ownership of someone else's victimization?

It is akin to the concept of stolen valor, in which someone pretends to have been in the military and to have faced the horrors of warfare, laying claim to something they never experienced in an attempt to be praised for their bravery and seen as some sort of hero.

They are using someone else's suffering for their personal gain. Race activists attempt to share in the victimization of those who experienced slavery and racial oppression in order to rationalize their own circumstances and demand that others do things for them. They are using someone else's suffering for their personal gain. Perhaps we can call this "stolen oppression."

It isn't just that people are engaging in this stolen oppression. They are taking the claims further than even those they are stealing from. I think about people like Booker T. Washington, a man who directly experienced slavery yet became educated and elevated himself despite it. He had no interest in excuses, believing that a man is wholly capable of making something of himself if he is willing to put in the effort. It is incredible that people alive today, who live among unprecedented abundance and opportunity, could feel more entitled to restitution than someone who was literally a slave. I wish it were possible to travel in time so that the people alive today could go back to the late 1800s and have the opportunity to let the former slaves know just how difficult their lives are. I am sure those former slaves would be sympathetic to their plight.

The Power of Education

In 1901, Washington published his autobiography, *Up from Slavery*. Washington focused heavily on education as a means of improving oneself and went on to establish and work with the Tuskegee Institute. Even from an early age, he understood that education was the key to elevating oneself. He recounted that as a child, while still in slavery, he saw children studying in a little schoolhouse and thought that being able to study in that way would be "like being admitted to paradise." He understood the importance of using education to make yourself useful to those around you so that you can lift yourself up, lift others up, and leave the world better than you found it.[2]

This is as true today as it was then. Children immersed in a culture of learning and discipline, respect, and personal responsibility, regardless of their circumstances, are much more likely to succeed than children who are not. Washington's mother, who was also a slave, was uneducated and illiterate, yet she still encouraged him to embrace education and did her best to help him learn to read and write. What an incredible mother she was. I also think about more contemporary examples like Dr. Ben Carson's mother—a single mother living in poverty who came from the foster care system and possessed only a third-grade education. The deck was stacked against her. However, she refused to allow her two sons to remain in those circumstances and encouraged them to take their education seriously. She made Ben and his brother check out and read two library books every week and write a report on one of them. (She would grade those reports, but later Ben would discover that his mother didn't actually know how to read and only pretended to grade them.) Thanks to this love and commitment, as well as her perseverance and prayerful guidance, Ben would go on to attend Yale and then the University of Michigan Medical School. He would eventually become a world-renowned pediatric neurosurgeon, and his brother would become a rocket scientist.

These are amazing stories of people harnessing the power of education and positive cultural attitudes and behaviors to propel themselves out of difficult circumstances. They did not make excuses or demand that others come to save them. They stood up and took responsibility for themselves. Children are almost always reliant on the adults in their lives to guide them into a culture that values such things. This cultural influence over outcomes has been demonstrated time and again. Extensive research on the effect of cultural behaviors, including a well-known study from the Brookings Institution, shows that of adults who finish high school, get a full-time job, and wait until they are twenty-one to get married and have children, only 2 percent remain in poverty.[3] It is clear that those who embrace a culture that values education, work ethic, personal responsibility, delayed gratification, kindness, respect, and an internal locus of control will be vastly more successful than those who embrace a culture that does not. Any culture that discourages these things—that disregards education, embraces blame-shifting, encourages promiscuity and fatherlessness, and promotes the idea that "someone or something else is responsible for what happens to me"—is a culture of failure, regardless of the race of those who subscribe to it. Anyone who is serious about helping people escape difficult circumstances should utterly reject it.

You will notice the stark contrast between this idea of cultural influence with an internal locus of control and structural determinism with an external locus of control. The idea that you have the power to control your own destiny is wholly rejected by Critical Race theorists. CRT, instead, suggests that your circumstances determine your outcomes and that these circumstances are driven by a system of white supremacy. There is no doubt that one's environment plays an influential role, but the idea that your outcomes depend on it outside of your own behavior and choices is outrageous. The United States of America is truly a land of opportunity. If a former slave can succeed in the postbellum South, I promise you, no matter what your race, you can do it, too.

The Mysticism of Race and Slavery

The way we approach discussions on slavery and race, in general, in America is often bizarre. It is treated with a sort of reverence and mysticism. It reminds me of Greek mythology and the way those stories were enshrined in the culture to the point of worship. The stories about slavery don't seem to involve real people or events anymore but seem more along the lines of the gods of Olympus going to battle with the Titans. There is a sense that before the slave trade existed, black people lived in some kind of non-white utopia that white colonizers decimated. There are stories about how black people in Africa had created an advanced civilization (not unlike Wakanda in *Black Panther*) which was stolen from them by white people who then exploited and enslaved them. Many black people still refer to each other as kings and queens, as if they are descended from some long-lost royal bloodline. The Five-Percent Nation, which has had a large influence on hip-hop music, including artists like Jay-Z and the Wu-Tang Clan, believe that black people are the gods of Earth and white people are devils. There are stories about how black people were able to see, hear, and smell things more than three miles away, but the food of the white man somehow weakened them. The belief seems to be that non-white people were superhumans who all lived together in harmony, prancing through meadows and singing songs of peace and love while riding around on unicorns until the white man showed up and started raining down fire and brimstone.

Never mind the brutality of Native American tribes toward each other throughout history. Never mind the brutality of African tribes toward each other throughout history. Never mind the barbarism rampant throughout the Middle East. Forget about the inhumane horrors the Aztecs committed in Mexico. Ignore the conquests and savagery in Asia, like that of Genghis Khan and the Mongol Empire. Only the pale-skinned Europeans engaged in any sort of violence and subjugation. History was full of nothing but rainbows and butterflies before evil white people decided to destroy it all.

Clearly, the world was not the peaceful utopia race activists pretend it was. The story of humanity is human beings doing awful things to each other. This is not specific to any race or people group. That includes slavery.

Slavery in America was not unique. It was an institution that had been around for thousands of years without any real moral controversy prior to the Enlightenment. It wasn't particularly remarkable that slavery existed in America, since it had existed all over the world for a long time prior. Most of the African slaves who were brought to America were sold into slavery by other Africans. Slavery existed in Africa long before any slave traders showed up on its coasts. Slavery in Africa and among Africans was not at all considered a moral abomination. This means that, while I am sure the enslaved did not particularly enjoy being slaves, they had no moral objection to the institution itself. They would just as soon have enslaved others if given the opportunity. This is the story of human history, even reaching as far back as biblical times, such as the Hebrew people being enslaved by the Egyptians during the time of Moses. Slavery still exists even today in many places in Africa and the Middle East and is perpetrated by non-white people. These facts, however, continue to be ignored.

Slavery was not unique to America, nor was it unique to black people. As Thomas Sowell often points out, nearly every people group from every culture throughout the world has been both the enslaved and the slave owners at some point in history.[4] That includes white people. The word "slave," itself, comes from the word "Slav" as a description of the Slavic people who were enslaved by Muslims in the ninth century. During the transatlantic slave trade, Barbary pirates captured Europeans and enslaved them in North Africa. White people were still being bought and sold in the Ottoman Empire long after slavery was abolished here in America. Why don't we teach this in our history classes? Why don't we consider this in our discussions of slavery? Why is slavery viewed with such a miniscule frame of reference, as if American slavery is the only kind that ever existed? The history of slavery is far more complex than what we are led to believe by race-hustling charlatans.

Even if we only look at America, slavery still was not as simple as it is made out to be. It is complicated by the indentured servitude of the Irish (which is often downplayed in conversations on slavery) and the fact that many slave owners in America were actually black themselves. Some of them had benevolent motives (e.g., purchasing family members), but there were plenty of others who owned slaves for purely economic reasons, no different than white slave owners. How does one reconcile that historical truth?

How do we contend with historical figures like William Ellison, a black slave owner in South Carolina who ran a nine hundred-acre cotton plantation and owned sixty-three slaves?[5] What are we to make of the fact that Ellison was one of 171 black slave owners in South Carolina alone, not to mention the approximately six thousand slave owners throughout the South during that period?[6] Do we ignore the fact that many black people like Ellison supported both the institution of slavery as well as the Confederacy during the Civil War?

Facts such as these are inconvenient for many Americans who want to cling to the mysticism surrounding American slavery and the idea that white people should be held responsible for it. They wish to use it as a scapegoat for all of our current social ills. We are bombarded with films and TV shows about slavery, slavery-inspired artwork and statues, and constant references to the institution being a cornerstone of the black identity and the current plight of black Americans. Yet, Booker T. Washington was only thirty-six years removed from its abolition when he wrote *Up from Slavery*, and he had no interest in looking backward—and certainly no interest in holding onto slavery as a crutch or excuse. He had no interest in hating slave owners or seeking vengeance. He had no interest in believing slavery held some kind of magical power over him or that he was incapable of moving forward because of what had happened a mere thirty-six years earlier. Now, here we are, over 150 years removed from the end of the Civil War and still blaming slavery for our inability to succeed. How does that make sense?

Internal vs. External Locus of Control

It is a bit of cruel irony that Booker T. Washington exemplified opposing victimhood and championed the pursuit of education and excellence, yet many of the schools that bear his name have abysmal outcomes which they blame on institutional racism and a lack of racial equity. For example, at Booker T. Washington High School in Tuskegee, Alabama, only 10 percent of students are proficient in math and only 25 percent are proficient in reading;[7] at Booker T. Washington High School in Atlanta, Georgia, only 7 percent of students are proficient in math and only 15 percent are proficient in reading;[8] and at Booker T. Washington Middle School in Baltimore, Maryland, less than 1 percent of students are proficient in either math or reading.[9]

All of the school systems in these examples have majority black student populations, black superintendents, and mostly black school boards. Their cities are all run by black mayors with majority black city councils. This would suggest that perhaps racism is not the actual problem. Maybe there are other variables at play that need to be examined. Some might claim that funding is the issue. But Baltimore City Schools spends more than $19,000 per student and still sees these horrendous outcomes.[10] Unfortunately, none of this seems to matter to those who are committed to blaming every negative thing associated with black people on the history of slavery and systemic racism.

A similar lesson can be learned from historically black colleges and universities (HBCUs). A 2018 study published by the *Atlanta Journal-Constitution* revealed that among twenty HBCUs in 2015, four out of every five incoming freshmen failed to earn a degree in six years. Some schools, like Arkansas Baptist College and Virginia University of Lynchburg, had graduation rates as low as 5 percent. By comparison, the national average was 59 percent.[11] Those schools are run by black administrators with predominantly black student bodies. Can we blame racism for their abysmal outcomes? What exactly are the racial barriers there? Those schools are in complete control of their systems. They often have much less stringent admission requirements so as to boost their enrollment and increase postsecondary opportunities for black students with lower GPAs and ACT/SAT scores. Consider that if a college admits a student who graduates from one of the terrible public schools that we previously discussed after having not met proficiency standards in math and reading, how likely are they to succeed at the university level? Whose fault is this? It would seem many things that have nothing to do with race can be blamed for these outcomes.

This brings us back to the idea of having an internal locus of control—believing you are in control of what happens to you. Booker T. Washington embraced this, and it is a big reason he was able to succeed even after having been enslaved. An internal locus of control places your own hands on the steering wheel of your life and says you have the ability to forge your own path. In conjunction with Ramsey Solutions, author Chris Hogan conducted a survey of ten thousand millionaires in 2017 and found that 97 percent of them believed they were in control of their own destinies. Many people believe that wealthy people inherited their money and that is the only reason they are wealthy, but Hogan's survey revealed that only 21 percent of those ten thousand millionaires inherited anything at all, and only 16 percent inherited more than $100,000. The vast majority of people who build wealth do so from practically nothing. According to Hogan, they do it by taking personal responsibility, practicing intentionality with their finances, being goal-oriented, working hard, and being consistent.[12]

These are the things we should be instilling in our children. Throw victimhood talk into the garbage. Lose the "someone else is responsible for my circumstances" victim mentality. Let go of the obsession with race and slavery both as a source of identity and as an excuse for failure. Teach children that success is well within their reach if they want it. We need to teach them the importance of education, having a work ethic, discipline, and personal responsibility. We need to teach them to have an internal locus of control and hold up people like Booker T. Washington as role models instead of people like Ibram X. Kendi. We need to teach our children that they absolutely have the power to shape their own destinies.

CHAPTER 12

The American Cultural Revolution

The most important thing is to be strong.
With strength, one can conquer others, and to conquer
others gives one virtue.

—Mao Zedong

See if any of this sounds familiar: A sociopolitical movement is initiated to purge society of its impure and oppressive history, the ill effects of which are said to still permeate all of its institutions. The people of the society are separated into proletariat victims and bourgeoisie oppressors, and those labeled "oppressors" are targeted for removal from systems of power to be replaced by those labeled as victims. There are demands to eliminate old customs, culture, habits, and ideas. Statues and other symbols that represent the old, oppressive society are torn down. Ideological enemies of the "new" are publicly humiliated and forced to confess and repent of their sins. Radical ideologues take over institutions. Children and young adults are targeted for ideological indoctrination and used as foot soldiers to advance the cause. There is violence in the streets against enemies of the ideology. There is a push for "equity" in institutions. Media and entertainment platforms are used to heavily push propaganda. Landlords, people on the political right, and capitalist sympathizers are all disparaged. Anyone who opposes the revolutionary principles of the ideology is labeled an enemy. Academic research papers are compromised by radical leftist ideology and vetted by people who adhere to that ideology before they are published; journalism is compromised by radical leftist ideology and reporters are required to follow the ideological narratives. Many people are bullied into activism and find themselves—out of either fear or a desire to belong—waving flags and shouting slogans for things they do not truly believe in and would not otherwise support. Ideological purity is a moving metric by which no one can truly be deemed pure enough or do enough right things to achieve purity, since "the right things" keep rapidly changing. There is zero tolerance for any opposition whatsoever to the given dogma, and as a result, families and friends are torn apart. Widespread uncertainty, fear, and distrust run rampant throughout society.

It certainly sounds as if I am describing the current state of America, doesn't it? But this is actually what happened during the Chinese Cultural Revolution under Mao Zedong, which ultimately ended up with tens of millions of people dying. The reason it seems familiar is because the implementation of ideas like Critical Race Theory (and Critical Theory, in general) are driven directly by Marxist ideals, and the subsequent outcomes are the same.

Mao was a Marxist, concerned with purging Chinese society of capitalist ideas and so-called "bourgeois" thinking. He is quoted as saying, "Before a brand-new social system can be built on the site of the old, the site must be swept clean."[1] Critical Race theorists, likewise, are concerned with destroying capitalist ideas and the liberal order, eliminating the "bourgeois" Western thinking that they call "whiteness," and tearing down and sweeping society clean of our old institutions so that new social systems can be built in their own image. It is not a coincidence that these things appear to be so similar. The blueprint for Critical Race Theory comes directly from Karl Marx.

CRT advocates will often push back against that statement. But it is clear for anyone who cares to examine it that CRT's Marxist foundation is intentional and undeniable. It is no accident that Patrisse Cullors, one of the founders of Black Lives Matter, proclaimed that she and the other founders (Alicia Garza and Opal Tometi) are trained Marxists. It is no accident that Cullors stated she was honored to have her book on racial activism compared to Mao's Little Red Book. It is no accident that Ibram X. Kendi claims that capitalism and racism are "conjoined twins" or that he wants to create an antiracism governing body to which all government and political entities will be subject, effectively creating an anticapitalist, antibourgeois (i.e., anti-white) dictatorship. It is no accident that the very name Critical Race Theory was chosen, knowing that Critical Theory was developed by self-proclaimed Marxists for the intent of "reexamining and revitalizing Marxism" in the Frankfurt School. It is no accident that both Richard Delgado and Kimberlé Crenshaw, two of the founders of CRT, explicitly stated that everyone who attended the initial meeting in which Crenshaw coined the term "Critical Race Theory" were all Marxists. These are not misunderstandings or misrepresentations. These are the very people who developed and who promote CRT telling us exactly who they are, proudly and explicitly. It needs to be made clear that Critical Race Theory is unequivocally rooted in the ideology of Karl Marx and aims to institute a race-based cultural revolution.

Critical Theory and Cultural Marxism

Encyclopedia Britannica defines Critical Theory as:

Marxist-inspired movement in social and political philosophy originally associated with the work of the Frankfurt

School. Drawing particularly on the thought of Karl Marx and Sigmund Freud, critical theorists maintain that a primary goal of philosophy is to understand and to help overcome the social structures through which people are dominated and oppressed.[2]

Sounds familiar, doesn't it? Once again, we see a mention of the Frankfurt School where Critical Theory was developed and from which Critical Race Theory is ultimately derived. Even a cursory examination of the world of Critical Race Theory will quickly reveal that the ideological line marches directly back to this school, to Critical Theory, and to Marxists like Herbert Marcuse and Max Horkheimer. Critical Theory (and subsequently Critical Race Theory) was and is nothing more than Marxism repackaged. It is impossible to separate the two. I won't spend a lot of time on the deeper history here, as it is extensive and a bit beyond the scope of this book, but I do recommend the work of James Lindsay of New Discourses, as he brilliantly dives into this history and connects the dots to form an analogy to a spear, with Critical Race Theory being the spearhead.[3]

It is worth noting, however, that the purpose of this spear, to paraphrase Lindsay, is to gore the side of Western civilization and open it up to a Marxist revolution. That is the most important point, in my opinion, as that is exactly what we see happening right now—not only with Critical Race Theory but with gender theory, queer theory, and feminism as well. The point here is that Critical Race Theory is not about teaching history. It's not really about equity or diversity. It's not really even about race or racism ultimately. It is about instituting a cultural revolution.

What else are we to make of a movement that explicitly states that it rejects the incrementalism and step-by-step progress made by the civil rights movement? What else are we to make of a movement that rejects the ideals of liberalism (e.g., individualism, freedom, and peace)? What are we to make of a movement that promotes the idea that the oppressed are somehow tricked into believing that they are free and that they must be awakened? This is truly the argument CRT activists make. Consider this direct quote from Özlem Sensoy and Robin DiAngelo in their book *Is Everyone Really Equal?*:

> The logic of individual autonomy that underlies liberal humanism (the idea that people are free to make indepen- dent rational decisions that determine their own fate) was viewed as a mechanism for keeping the marginalized in their place by obscuring larger structural systems of inequality. In other words, it fooled people into believing that they had more freedom and choice than society struc- tures actually allowed.[4]

Again, we see these ideas of structural determinism surfacing in the literature—ideas that are decidedly Marxist in their reasoning and application. Sensoy and DiAngelo explicitly say they oppose the idea that "people are free to make independent rational decisions that determine their own fate." They claim the oppressive system is in control at all times and even has the ability to fool people into believ- ing they actually have personal autonomy. The system has the ability to hide oppression within the folds of the status quo and the everyday operations of society and its institutions to the point of complete invisibility, until the oppressed are no longer even aware that they are being oppressed.

All of this means CRT advocates believe non-white people must actively be made to be conscious of their plight—that they are cur- rently asleep, trapped in the Matrix, unaware that they are being fed a false illusion of peace and freedom. In reality, they are slaves who

must be awakened to the horrors of their oppression in order to recognize their victimhood. Individualism, freedom, peace, and even the
idea of rights are all tools to maintain the status quo and keep the
oppressed in a perpetual state of slumber, oblivious to just how terrible
their lives really are. They must become *woke*, reject "incrementalism
and step-by-step progress," and thus revolt. The goal is revolution.

White people, likewise, must be made aware of how they are
oppressing others simply by existing and living their lives. They must be
made to recognize that promoting ideas like liberty and equality before
the law only promotes the status quo of white supremacy and marginal-
izes minority groups. They, too, must be awakened and actively work to
dismantle these systems of whiteness through revolution.

This is Marxism—or, some may say, neo-Marxism or cultural
Marxism—in action. Therefore, it seems sensible to look at the outcomes of applied Marxism around the world and the outcomes of
Marxist-inspired revolutions to examine the validity and efficacy of
such ideas. Not surprisingly, in every single example, there has been
widespread destruction and chaos. There are zero examples of Marxism
yielding positive outcomes. It has ended in catastrophe every time.

Frank Dikötter, a Dutch historian who has extensively studied
the Chinese Cultural Revolution under Mao, described its tragic and
traumatic aftermath by writing, "It was about loss—a loss of trust,
loss of friendship, loss of faith in other human beings, loss of predict-
ability in social relationships."[5] Friends were turned against friends.
Family members were turned against family members. Neighbors
would turn on their neighbors. Children would spy on their parents.
It was Orwellian, psychological warfare and emotional manipulation
that pitted people against each other, destroying their sense of
humanity. Mao believed that disorder and chaos were desirable, and
so thrust China directly into that. He left tens of millions of dead
bodies in his wake—a number that is difficult to pin down exactly

because of the sheer number of violent deaths and the millions who also died from starvation during the Great Leap Forward. Regardless, it is safe to say that multiple millions of people died and there was widespread devastation as a direct result of Mao and his poisonous ideology. Marxist ideas are consistent in this regard. Everywhere they are implemented, they invariably leave behind a horrific trail of death and destruction. They always end in disorder and chaos.

What, then, might the result be here in America if we allow this spear to rip apart our institutions, turning friends against friends and family against family—something we have already seen happening? What might result if we allow ourselves to lose faith in our fellow human beings, to lose trust, to lose a sense of connectedness in shared history, values, and culture? What happens if we normalize violence against our political opponents? What will result from allowing the four "olds"—old customs, old culture, old ideas, and old habits—to be eliminated? What if we give way to "lived experience" and reject objective truth? What happens when we instill the concept of Antonio Gramsci's cultural hegemony and pit "the oppressed" against their "capitalist oppressors"? What happens if we embrace CRT's assertion that the appearance of progress in race relations is a farce that merely hides racism? What kind of society will our children inherit if we raise the next generation to be consumed with anger, grievance, paranoia, suspicion, vengefulness, and to view themselves as perpetual victims? What is the outcome of such a religion?

Religious Extremism

In *God in the Dock*, C. S. Lewis wrote,

Of all tyrannies, a tyranny sincerely exercised for the good of its victims may be the most oppressive. It would be better to live under robber barons than under omnipotent moral busybodies. The robber baron's cruelty may sometimes sleep, his cupidity may at some point be satiated; but those who torment us for our own good will torment us without end for they do so with the approval of their own conscience. They may be more likely to go to heaven yet at the same time likelier to make a Hell of earth. This very kindness stings with intolerable insult. To be "cured" against one's will and cured of states which we may not regard as disease is to be put on a level of those who have not yet reached the age of reason or those who never will; to be classed with infants, imbeciles, and domestic animals.[6]

This is Critical Race Theory. Lewis called those who practice such things moral busybodies. I call them religious extremists. Theirs is the type of dogmatic thinking that asserts the ends justify the means and that things should be done "for the greater good." Those who subscribe to this religion believe these things should not only be done, but that they, as the anointed priests and evangelists, have some kind of divine right to decide when and how they are done and that everyone else must be subject to their whims. Individualism and freedom are their enemies. They believe that they, alone, know what is best and that the people must be made (through governmental force) to adhere to this infallible utopian vision. They believe that they, alone, can see the truth and the rest of us are simply blinded by our sinful natures. Therefore, we must be made to bow to their gods, to worship at their altar, and to be baptized in their faith in order to elevate our own consciousness, throw off the chains of oppression, and establish paradise. We must be made to repent of our sins and be born again— leaving behind our old selves, our old culture, our old ways of "knowing," wiping the slate clean, and stepping into a new, fully conscious existence. There is no choice. This cannot be left to free will. It must be done, and it must be controlled. Resistance to conversion, blasphemous speech and thoughts, apostasy—these are not to be tolerated. Blasphemers and heretics are to be publicly shamed and sent away for reeducation. The purity of the church requires completely purging the stain of sin from the world—for the greater good. Critical Race Theory is an extremist religion.

It is interesting that these Marxist ideologies bear such remarkable similarities to the practices of religious extremism. It gives us tremendous insight into what the Founding Fathers were talking about when they went to great lengths to protect religious freedom by ratifying the First Amendment of the Constitution. The prospect of being forced to submit to a state religion was a primary issue they sought to avoid. Many of the colonists who had come to America from England were fleeing exactly that sort of religious persecution. The First Amendment was directly intended to prevent such a thing from taking place in America—yet here we are, being subjected to the religion of progressivism being handed down by the state. However, because progressivism is not technically considered a religion, it is able to slither through the loophole in the First Amendment to use the government as its ideological enforcer.

It should be clear, regardless, that religious freedom means the government should not impose any kind of ideological dogma on the citizenry. That would effectively be stomping on the beliefs and freedoms of the people. The Founding Fathers knew how that ends, and so do we. We've seen how it ends all throughout history. Attempting to use the power of the government to force people to adhere to the dogmatic moral framework, beliefs, and practices of one's particular ideology is undoubtedly the road to tyranny and societal collapse. It's no wonder Critical Race Theory is so hostile to the First Amendment.

It often baffles me that we Americans tend to be so arrogant about our ability to resist the destruction that has dismantled societies around the globe where ideological viruses have been allowed to spread. We recognize their failures in the Soviet Union, Cambodia, Venezuela, Cuba, Maoist China, etc. We recognize the substantial problems with radical Islam running governments in the Middle East and infringing on the liberty of its people in the name of ideology. Yet we somehow believe we are too enlightened for those things to ever happen here.

Marxism is repackaged into Critical Theory, and people somehow believe they have stumbled upon something different and new. They believe they are right, that they are morally justified, and therefore, forcing their ideas onto others is righteous. The result is that an entire generation is being raised to believe these toxic ideas have never been tried before (let alone that they have led to horrific atrocities every time), that they are somehow being secretly oppressed, and that they somehow have the power and moral authority to tear down these supposed systems of oppression and build new ones without any short- or long-term consequences whatsoever. This generation is being systematically led down a path of utter destruction. People who succumb to the siren song of Marxism, in whatever form it takes, believe that they truly know what's best for all 330 million people who live in this country, and that they will get it right this time. It just wasn't done correctly elsewhere. It was misguided. It was co-opted. It was undermined. The American Cultural Revolution will be different. Don't worry, folks. This time it will work.

CHAPTER 13

Gratitude and Perspective

*And we know that all things work together for good
to those who love God, to those who are the called
according to His purpose.*

—Romans 8:28

Imagine a man crawling through the desert, exhausted and dehydrated, dragging himself along and doing everything he can to cling to life. Miraculously, just when he thinks he can't possibly go any further, he comes upon an oasis. He plunges his face in the water and drinks deeply, thinking that this water is the greatest, most precious thing in the entire world. That water would be sacred to him. Now imagine someone who lives on an island in the middle of a lake who has running water in his house and even special water filters. It is nearly certain that water would not have anywhere close to the same value to that person as it does to the man in the desert. In fact, he might even grow to be sick of water, completely taking it for granted.

When we are surrounded by abundance, we can lose our sense of gratitude and perspective. In those situations, we must be intentional about reminding ourselves just how blessed we really are. When people are dealing with stress and dissatisfaction, some therapists will have them keep a gratitude journal, detailing all the things they are thankful for. This practice keeps them centered and their lives in perspective. Marriages collapse because couples forget why they fell in love and begin to take each other for granted—many even stepping out on their spouse with another person. They completely lose their sense of gratitude and perspective. People struggle with "keeping up with the Joneses," try to cling to celebrity trends, get addicted to plastic surgery to make themselves look more attractive, portray themselves as something they are not on social media, or all of the above because they forget to be grateful. Americans are constantly struggling to get whatever they don't have while simultaneously taking precious little time to appreciate the things they already do have. Actor Jim Carrey once said, "I wish people could realize all their dreams in wealth and fame so that they could see that it's not where you're going to find your sense of completion."[1]

We search for meaning as human beings. If we feel like we lack purpose, we will instinctively seek it out somewhere. Some people think meaning is found in how much money they have; some think it is found in their possessions; some think it is found in status and popularity; some think it is found in attractiveness and beauty; some think it is found in sex; some think it is found in power. As Christians, we still struggle with these things like any fallible person, but we know that true meaning and purpose can be found only in God. There is a God-sized hole in each of us that we desperately try to fill with all of these other things, never finding fulfillment and peace. Because no matter how hard we try, we just can't fill it on our own.

I am aware that not everyone will agree with that, even if they agree with the overall message of this book. That's okay. The point stands, even for an atheist: The search for meaning is pointless if we lack gratitude and perspective. We will seek meaning in all the wrong places. Jordan Peterson often says that happiness is a result, not a goal. He says we should not pursue happiness but meaning.[2] I would take that further and say we cannot pursue meaning until we embrace gratitude.

I like the word "contentment" because I think it encapsulates the whole point: If you are content, you are not just happy; you are at peace with your life. Happiness, to me, is just a fleeting emotion. You can watch my favorite comedian, Brian Regan, do a stand-up routine and feel happy for a moment, even if your life outside the theater is chaos. But contentment suggests that all is as it should be.

So why am I talking about gratitude and perspective in a book about Critical Race Theory? Quite simply, because CRT is born directly from a profound lack of both. It promotes hatred and resentment for our country, our institutions, our history, our traditions, and our values, claiming that they are all tainted by racial bigotry. There is no sense of gratitude. There is only grievance.

The founders of CRT and those who adhere to it are desperately searching for meaning and purpose. That's what makes Critical Race Theory so attractive. It is a substitute for religious belief—whether that takes the form of power, status, money, or establishing one's place in the world. I mentioned earlier that race activists romanticize the past and view themselves as reincarnations of historical heroes. They engage in a sort of live-action role-play, rejecting reality in favor of some fantasy where they play the part of the oppressed, heroically running into battle against the evil oppressor. Like the person who lives in the middle of a lake with running water and fancy filtration systems, all the blessings that we have in this country are completely invisible and taken for granted. They cannot be acknowledged because that would undercut their claims of oppression. Once their immense blessings are recognized, it is difficult for others to take the tragic character they play seriously. It's like a wealthy celebrity who claims to be oppressed because the temperature of his Olympic-sized indoor pool is a few degrees too cold. The pool temperature might truly be a problem that needs to be addressed, but to ignore all the good things you have and pretend that this problem somehow makes you a victim is asinine. That is, if the problem is even real. The foolishness is especially true if the problem is imaginary.

The Story of Joseph

A sense of gratitude is vital for staying grounded, even in the face of true hardships. I think a lot about the biblical story of Joseph. His own siblings hated him so much that they threw him into a pit and then sold him into bondage. Can there be anything worse than that? As if that weren't enough, he was later thrown into prison after his master's wife lied and accused him of trying to rape her (even though she was the one who tried to seduce him). He was left in prison for years; eventually he met Pharaoh's former cupbearer and former baker there. He interpreted dreams for each of them, telling the cupbearer he would be restored to his position and the baker that he would be hanged. Both those things came to pass.

The cupbearer promised to tell Pharoah about Joseph when he was released from prison, but he forgot—until one day a few years later, when Pharoah couldn't find anyone capable of interpreting his disturbing dreams. Joseph was released, and his interpretation of Pharaoh's dreams, which warned of a coming famine—and wise advice about how to prepare for and survive it—impressed Pharaoh so deeply that he gave Joseph command of all of Egypt, second only to himself.

Joseph was tasked with making sure enough food was stored up so that people would not go hungry during the famine. Eventually Joseph's brothers, who had sold him into slavery, came to Egypt to buy grain. Joseph tests them to see if they have truly changed, and the family ultimately reunites and reconciles.

I recount that story to make this point: Joseph did not harbor resentment toward his brothers, nor did he demand restitution for what they had done to him. He was grateful to have his family back and for the good that God had brought out of the situation. He said,

> "But now, do not therefore be grieved or angry with your-selves because you sold me here; for God sent me before you to preserve life. For these two years the famine has been in the land, and there are still five years in which there will be neither plowing nor harvesting. And God sent me before you to preserve a posterity for you in the earth, and to save your lives by a great deliverance." (Genesis 45:5–7)

What Joseph went through was awful. It was unjust. It was evil. He was truly victimized. There is no denying that. But if none of it had happened, he never would have been put in a position to warn of the impending famine, and he never would have been able to help Egypt prepare for it. Many Egyptians would have died. His own family would have died. There has to be some gratitude for that.

Now, I want to make sure I am clear in saying this isn't to suggest that what happened to Joseph was good in itself, that it should be celebrated, or that bad things in general should be praised. But one thing we often discuss as Christians is God's ability to bring good out of bad situations. That doesn't justify or rationalize the bad, but it does say that these things do not have to lead to bad outcomes. For example, a child conceived in rape can be a blessing to a family and can grow up to do amazing things, despite the horrific circumstances that brought her into existence. That was the case for Layne Beachley: she was conceived in rape and given up for adoption rather than aborted. She grew up to be a world champion surfer, has been inducted into both the Australian and American surfing halls of fame, and has launched a foundation that provides scholarships and mentoring for young women in Australia. This was also the case for my own sister-in-law, Tiffany Johnson, who was attacked by a shark while she and my brother were snorkeling in the Bahamas; as a result, she lost part of her arm. This was clearly a devastating and traumatic event. But because of this, she has been invited to go on major television shows, has traveled the country to tell her story, and has launched a full-time ministry about the goodness of God that is blessing, impacting, and inspiring millions of people—all because she was attacked by that shark.

Sometimes, going through difficult times gives us the wisdom to be able to help others. This can be tough to consider, because it might sound like being grateful for rape, shark attacks, or whatever other awful thing might happen to a person. But actually, it is about having gratitude for life itself, and for the fact that good things truly can come from bad events.

In the same way, slavery in our country was a terrible thing. But without it, I would not be here. Some of my ancestors, like Joseph, were sold into bondage by their kinsmen and forced to endure hardships while they were stripped of their freedom and their humanity. Because of that evil, I have been blessed to be born into the greatest country in the world, into a land of abundance and opportunity. Should I spit on that because of what happened in the past? Should I embrace grievance and victimhood instead of acknowledging the tremendous blessings I have?

Positive Psychology

Two of my favorite animated TV series are *Avatar: The Last Airbender* and its follow-up, *Avatar: The Legend of Korra*. In both, a character named Uncle Iroh serves as the wise old man archetype. In *Legend of Korra*, he tells the main character, "If you look for the light, you will often find it. But if you look for the dark, that is all you will ever see."[3] This is a profound truth. It speaks to the fact that we have the power to shape our own realities, either positively or negatively. Negativity has a way of overshadowing everything, regardless of how much good there is. Psychology has shown that our brains are more likely to remember and be influenced by negative events than positive ones even when the positive events heavily outweigh the negative. This is called negativity bias. Because of this, we often have to be intentional about being positive and consciously look for things to be thankful for. This is why many motivational speakers focus on positive thinking and gratitude. This is why Martin Seligman, one of the researchers behind the concept of "learned helplessness," wrote a book called *Learned Optimism*, in which he offers techniques on how to enhance one's quality of life through the power of positive thinking and finding the good in a given situation.[4]

How foolish and arrogant it is to reject any sense of gratitude for the immense blessing it is to live in the United States of America, to look back on our history with our noses in the air, believing ourselves to be more righteous and enlightened than our predecessors. How spoiled and narcissistic do you have to be to scoff at the Founding Fathers and the Constitution they created, believing yourself to be morally and intellectually superior to those who made the life you are living today possible? How delusional do you have to be to denigrate the system of capitalism that has not only provided you with the exceptional standard of living you currently enjoy, but has vastly reduced global poverty by substantially improving the standard of living for people all over the world? How insufferable and disrespectful to take a gift that is given to you—the gift that is America, the gift of liberty obtained through struggle, blood, sacrifice, and countless heroes giving their lives to make sure you could have it—and just throw it away as if it isn't good enough. How dare you!

This certainly does not mean that we cannot address and solve problems—but it does require us to approach those problems with a sense of perspective. The uber-rich celebrity with the Olympic-sized indoor pool may, indeed, have a problem with the temperature, and no one would suggest he isn't allowed to fix that. But how senseless is it to ignore the immense blessing of even having such a pool in the first place? Would it make sense for him to complain that his neighbor has a nicer pool without temperature problems and paint himself as a victim? Should he burn his multimillion-dollar mansion to the ground in protest? Should he burn his neighbor's home to the ground?

Of course, we would roll our eyes at such antics and say that person is crazy and out of touch. Americans claiming to be victimized simply because someone else has something they don't is exactly the same.

Generally speaking, even beyond the racial elements, many people in the United States have no idea just how rich they are. There is much talk about the wealthy 1 percent, but many Americans fail to recognize that if they make just $34,000 per year that they, themselves, are in the top 1 percent globally.[5] They don't recognize that they are some of the richest people in the entire world because their perspective is skewed by relativity. They think that because someone across town has more than they do, they are somehow being victimized. It is the fixed-pie fallacy—the belief that the wealth pie is fixed and that as someone gains more wealth, it necessarily means that others must lose the same amount. Therefore, when you see someone else with more, you feel slighted and believe that something has been taken from you. It's nonsense. The truth is that the pie can always expand into an even bigger pie, and when that happens, everyone's standard of living increases. Consider the skyrocketing wealth of someone like Jeff Bezos. Regardless of what you think of him, Amazon has increased the standard of living for everyone in this nation by increasing choices, lowering costs, and making things more accessible, and has facilitated the operations of other businesses which also build wealth and increase our standard of living. The rising tide lifts all ships, as the saying goes.

We ultimately have much to be thankful for. Ideologies of grievance do not serve us well on any level. They are toxic and destructive. Any psychologist (who has not been poisoned by progressive indoctrination) will acknowledge how detrimental it is for a person to live in the past, to constantly compare themselves to others, to harbor a victim mentality, to have a profound lack of gratitude, to embrace an external locus of control, and to dwell on negativity. Psychology tells us that these things lead directly to poor outcomes. So why would we promote them? If they are toxic outside of issues of race, why would they magically benefit us within them?

We have to stop doing this to ourselves, and we must break the generational curse by refusing to teach our children to do it. History is messy. It is full of humans doing terrible things to each other. Every single person alive could find something in their family lineage to claim a grievance about if they wanted to. Every single person could find victimization in their family tree. But it does us no good to dwell on these things. We can't change the past. It's over. We can only take hold of the present and look to the future. We cannot abandon our gratitude and perspective. We must remain aware of and acknowledge the immense blessings that we have been given and how incredibly fortunate we are to live in a country like the United States of America. We don't have to have a holiday or a parade to give thanks for the terrible things that happened in the past, but the truth is that none of us would be here if history had not played out exactly as it did.

We have to recognize that, despite its scars, we are unbelievably blessed to live in a country that so many others are desperate to come to. Too many focus on these scars as evidence of victimhood and oppression, but our scars are what make our country great, not what make it broken. Our scars are what give us beauty. They are reminders, not of being victims, but of being victors. They are reminders of what we, as a nation, have endured and overcome. They are reminders of our strength and fortitude. They are reminders that good truly can come from bad.

CHAPTER 14

Colorblindness vs. CRT

*I have a dream that my four little children will one day
live in a nation where they will not be judged by the color
of their skin but by the content of their character.*

—Martin Luther King Jr.

Merriam-Webster tells us a paradigm shift is "an important change
that happens when the usual way of thinking about or doing
something is replaced by a new and different way." It occurs when the
people in a society recognize their assumptions and behaviors are
flawed. As a result, that society changes its course. When scientists
discovered that Earth is indeed a globe and not flat, as was previously
thought, a fundamental paradigm shift took place concerning how
societies thought about and navigated the world. In the same way, our
society is long overdue in realizing that our assumptions and behaviors
surrounding race are extremely flawed. It is time we initiate a paradigm
shift and forever alter our navigation systems.

As I look at our country and see the rapidly growing polarization,
tribalism, and intolerance of different viewpoints, I wonder how long
we can endure without a radical change of course. How long can a
nation continue to exist if its people are so sharply divided that they
see themselves as disparate, competing groups incapable of sharing a

common history, philosophy, and culture? Does the phrase *E Pluribus Unum* mean, "out of many, one" or does it mean, "out of one, many"?

Thanks to ideologies like Critical Race Theory, we see a purposeful divisiveness flooding our sociopolitical atmosphere with race as the spearhead. Why would any reasonable person want to continue on a path where so much of society is being intentionally and aggressively filtered through the lens of race? We know that throughout history, racial categorization has always been used as a weapon to drive division and enmity. Why would we, as a society, want to perpetuate that? At what point do we recognize the clear toxicity of grouping each other into skin-based collectives?

"I have a dream that my four little children will one day live in a nation where they will not be judged by the color of their skin but by the content of their character." This oft-quoted line from Dr. Martin Luther King Jr.'s "I Have a Dream" speech continues to resonate nearly sixty years later. It reminds us of the irrationality, cruelty, and inhumanity that underlie the racial segregation of human beings. It is a call for unity, a call for brotherhood and sisterhood, a call to release our self-crippling grip on the past and to move forward together as one. It seems incredible that such inspirational and seemingly uncontroversial notions could ever be met with anger and hostility. But they are.

When Dr. King first spoke those words, there was, indeed, anger and hostility emanating from those who would have preferred to remain segregated and to continue living as perpetually divided peoples. Now we see similar negative reactions when anyone suggests de-emphasizing race to unite as unhyphenated Americans. Today's anger and hostility is very much like the anger and hostility back then, and it exists for the same reasons. Those who fight on the side of racial identity today also seem to wish to continue living as divided people. Haven't we seen enough of this throughout history to know what often results when certain groups place too much value on race? Has it not been a driving force for enmity, resulting in wars, slavery, and genocide?

I have asked myself many questions like these over the years—questions that apparently are considered taboo and heretical. Asking them publicly has earned me and others general contempt and such loving names as "Uncle Tom" from those who believe that exploring such "dangerous" ideas is akin to racial treason. These are the people who cling to race with the kind of religious fanaticism that will not tolerate any blasphemy. However, I remain unmoved by such empty criticism and emotional reasoning. These are questions that demand answers. Why do we need race? What is the benefit of clinging to it? What would happen if we abandoned it? Do I have more in common with my white family members who live in the same rural town that I do, or with black strangers who live in some far-off city in a different state? What does it actually mean to be "black" beyond a mere physical description? What does it mean to be "white"? If it was wrong to categorize whole groups of people by race in the past, why is it not wrong to continue to do so today?

It often seems like the only reason we continue to do certain things is habit. We don't usually give much thought to why we do them or why we should continue to do them. Ironically, slavery used to be one of those things, before a paradigm shift took place. As we discussed, it had existed for thousands of years all over the world, with all manner of peoples being both slaves and slaveowners, before it ever came to our shores. Few people questioned it or critically examined its moral implications; it was simply the way things worked. It was the way things had always been. Not until people began asking questions did the walls of slavery began to crack and crumble. A moral abomination that had existed for thousands of years was brought to its knees because some people decided to go against the grain, to challenge the prevailing narrative, and to ask *why*. They initiated a paradigm shift.

So I am now also asking *why*. Why should we continue to give race such importance and divide ourselves into separate categories? When we treat race as the defining characteristic of who a person is in America, we can have no other outcome than the disastrous ones we saw in the past. It can only end with pain and suffering.

What Does Colorblindness Mean?

The idea of colorblindness directly opposes the philosophy of Critical Race Theory. Oftentimes, bad-faith actors express disdain for the idea of colorblindness and misrepresent its intentions. They erect nonsensical strawman arguments to attack, such as the idea that colorblindness means being physically unable to see color and pretending everyone looks, acts, and thinks the same way. This is, of course, ridiculous. No one advocating colorblindness means they can't physically see color; they mean that they see it and it doesn't matter. It has no bearing on how they treat others. I have had far too many conversations with progressives and even some race-obsessed conservatives who simply refuse to understand this perspective. They prefer to launch into a grand battle of disingenuity against this imaginary argument. It is the height of intellectual dishonesty to pretend not to understand what people mean when they say they embrace colorblindness and express a desire to move into a post-racial society.

Even well-meaning conservatives sometimes balk at the phrase, likely influenced by the bad-faith arguments. Voddie Baucham, a theologian whom I deeply respect, has argued against it, criticizing the use of the term in a 2019 talk he gave on ethnic gnosticism.[1] But he, too, misstated the argument. His point was that God loves variety; therefore, we should celebrate our differences and not try to homogenize everyone. (This is a semantic argument over terminology. This is fine, I suppose. We can be pedantic about it and pick a less metaphorical term so that people don't take it so literally.) But Baucham does recognize what people mean by the term "colorblindness." Why would we take issue with the terminology if we know what it means? I believe others also recognize what the term means and only pretend to take it literally.

Nobody is arguing for ignoring culture or variability. Nobody is pretending we are all exactly the same or that we should ignore our differences. Colorblindness simply means ignoring collectivist notions of race and, instead, embracing the uniqueness of each individual. People who are racially colorblind see the color of your skin the same way they see the color of your eyes and the color of your hair. They notice it. It just doesn't matter. It tells them nothing about who you are as a human being. Just as I can tell nothing about a person based on their eye color, neither can I tell anything about them based on their skin color. That is colorblindness.

Like CRT, colorblindness is a worldview. But unlike CRT, it rejects racial collectivism, collective guilt and collective victimhood, the idea that the group is more important than the individual, the demand that we view the world and everyone in it through an entirely racial lens, and the idea that racism can effectively be fought with more racism. It is the antithesis of Critical Race Theory. Colorblindness seeks to fulfill the promise of the civil rights movement, to elevate the individual above the group, and to judge them by the content of their character, not the color of their skin.

Victims and Saviors

Earlier, we discussed the romanticization of America's racial history, which creates a seemingly impenetrable wall that holds up racial grievance in perpetuity. For many, race is considered too important to abandon. The argument is generally that others (meaning "white people") will continue to see black people as black and make unfair judgments based on race; therefore, it is a pipe dream to consider that moving into a post-racial society is even possible. They simply refuse to be colorblind because they think others won't be.

I find that argument to be foolish and myopic. It reads more like an excuse than a rebuttal. It reminds me of a child's reasoning for why he cannot possibly do his chores: "I'm tired" or "There is too much to do" or "It will just get dirty again." None of these excuses are rational. They are all merely substitutes for the true statement, which is "I don't want to." I suspect this often is what is happening when people push back against colorblindness and unleash all manner of viciousness against its ideals. The arguments they present, if we are even to call them that, are nothing more than substitutes for the true statement: "I don't want to."

The question, then, is why do so many people have such an intense desire to cling to race? Why is it so important to keep it alive in our society? Why is there such animosity toward and resistance to colorblindness?

There is an easy answer for those in power or those who seek it, as we have already highlighted: They directly benefit from it. They have personal and financial incentives to perpetuate racial grievances, real or contrived, as well as incentives to oppose anything that will eliminate them. It isn't even clear that the people in power actually believe in the foolishness they promote, but they have no problem using it to manipulate others. To them, it is vitally important that obsession with racial identity and perceptions of widespread racism and injustice continue to persist because, without them, there is no need for their so-called "expertise." As Upton Sinclair said, "It is difficult to get a man to understand something when his salary depends on him not understanding it."[2]

There is, however, another group of people who truly buy into the race ideology and the snake oil of Critical Race Theory, and they are the foot soldiers those in power easily manipulate. When they are told they are victims of white supremacy and that racism explains any negative outcomes in their lives, they believe it. They cling to race as their defining characteristic, harbor vitriol toward racial outgroups (and anyone else who doesn't toe the line), believe in perpetual racial grievance, and believe their ancestors' suffering is their own. They believe racism is everywhere and that they are truly oppressed in the United States of America.

I have often pondered the reasons for this. Typically, when I challenge the idea that black Americans are currently oppressed, other black people whose race forms the core of their identity immediately respond with animosity. They accuse me of hating black people, of being an Uncle Tom and a race traitor, or say I possess some form of self-hatred. This behavior, of course, helps support my racial grievance hypothesis. Many people view an attack on the idea of systemic oppression as an attack on their very identities. If grievance is removed, they will no longer have meaning or purpose. They won't know who they are. Their entire sense of self is wholly centered around slavery, Jim Crow, the word "nigger," and the general concept of racial discrimination and white hate. Being black, for them, is synonymous with being oppressed. This hypothesis would make sense of why so many people despise the idea of colorblindness. Colorblindness removes not only the toxic practice of assigning collective guilt but also their ability to claim collective victimhood, which is a direct threat to their identity.

Likewise, some people buy into the race ideology from the other side and believe themselves to be saviors. They believe they have benefitted from white privilege and systemic racism while people like me have been crushed under the weight of this racial oppression. They believe it is their righteous duty and responsibility to dismantle these things in their own lives, in mine, and anywhere else they possibly can. Ironically, they also respond with animosity and vitriol when I challenge this notion. They are the embodiment of the internet meme that shows a pale-skinned person with a hand over the mouth of a dark-skinned person with the caption, "You poor, ignorant, stupid fool who has internalized white supremacy and racism—don't worry, I'll fight the good fight for you, since you are obviously too brainwashed to know better. I'll be offended on your behalf!"

Neither of these groups want anything whatsoever to do with colorblindness. Their identities depend on that idea being utterly crushed.

The George Floyd Incident

After George Floyd died, there was a massive nationwide race-based movement that painted all black people as victims of white oppression, particularly oppression by white police officers. The fact that there was no evidence that Floyd's arrest and death had anything to do with race whatsoever was immaterial. It symbolized the apparent oppression that black people supposedly face daily, and Derek Chauvin symbolized the evils of white supremacy that perpetuate this oppression. For many, it was an opportunity to reinforce their identities as victims or saviors. Even if they hadn't been personally victimized themselves, they were able to attach their identity to Floyd's, to make his experience their own, and demand that we all view it through the lens of race.

In a colorblind society, no one would have been able to accomplish that. In a colorblind society, the respective races of George Floyd and Derek Chauvin would have been irrelevant, unless there was compelling evidence to suggest otherwise. The event would have been discussed and covered by the media for what it was: a police officer restraining a drugged-out criminal who was resisting arrest that ended with the criminal passing away. The nature of the restraint could certainly be debated, and a jury might still have weighed it to determine whether there was any wrongdoing, but it almost certainly would not have turned into the national spectacle that it did, complete with protests and deadly riots. Race would have had nothing to do with it.

In 2016, police officers in Dallas, Texas, restrained thirty-two-year-old Tony Timpa in a similar manner as George Floyd, and Timpa also died during the arrest. But there was very little discussion about it at the time. In fact, most people didn't even hear about it until four years later when Floyd died, and someone pointed out that Timpa had died in a similar fashion. It doesn't take much analysis to figure out why the media treated Timpa and Floyd so differently: both Timpa and the police officers who arrested him were white.

Additionally, the media heavily focused on the fact that Floyd died under the knee of a white officer—but that officer was not the only cop on the scene. They widely ignore the others involved with Floyd's arrest—one of whom was of Asian descent and one of whom was black. Why? Not only were they both non-white, but they would have contributed the most to his death if it had truly stemmed from suffocation. As a speech-language pathologist, I can say unequivocally that Floyd's ability to constantly yell while he was under Chauvin's knee indicates his trachea was not compressed. Had it been, he would have had difficulty making any sound at all, let alone yell. If he died from asphyxiation, it would have been from not getting enough oxygen into his lungs due to pressure on his back. Since his trachea was not compressed, asphyxiation would have only occurred if he was unable to contract his diaphragm and expand his chest. So, if asphyxiation was the true cause of Floyd's death, it would have been from having someone on his back—not his neck.

Given those facts, if the people who continue to use Floyd's death as a call for justice are truly concerned about justice, why only focus on the white officer? Why are the anatomical and physiological facts about the trachea and vocal cords ignored? I'm not saying those other officers are guilty of anything, but it certainly seems strange to disregard them completely. Then there are all the other facts that are ignored, such as the bodycam footage showing Floyd was erratic and combative, that the police seemed to do everything they could to get him to calm down and into the police cruiser, that Floyd was yelling he couldn't breathe before anyone ever touched him, that he had a history of swallowing drugs (sometimes overdosing) to avoid being caught with them, and that he, himself, told officers to put him on the ground. Those facts are also irrelevant. Many people who remain outraged about Floyd's death aren't even aware of them.

It is apparent from the response to these details that the actual circumstances and facts surrounding George Floyd's death do not matter to race activists. What does matter is that he was black, and Derek Chauvin was white. This is also the case in the police shootings of Breonna Taylor, Rayshard Brooks, Jacob Blake, Ma'Khia Bryant, etc. The only variable many consider relevant is race. This is how a society driven by Critical Race Theory ideology operates.

But a colorblind society discourages such obsession with seeing all situations, relationships, and scenarios through the lens of race. That also means a colorblind society discourages seeing everything through a lens of racial grievance. As such, it is clear that someone who sees utility, or worse, necessity in maintaining racial identity through collective victimhood and collective guilt would inherently oppose any effort to remove it.

This is tragic. Many of the people who march, protest, and demand that they not be treated as a monolithic racial group simultaneously demand that we continue to view each other as monolithic racial groups. They constantly and hypocritically bemoan racism in society while also engaging in racism by making snap judgments and assigning guilt or innocence to others based solely on their skin color. Obsession with racial identity inevitably leads us down the dark and shadowy path of racial enmity. This does not mean we need to abandon our heritage or that we cannot be proud of our ancestry. It also does not mean we should ignore acts of actual racism. But it makes little sense to use race as a wall of separation between ourselves and our fellow countrymen—unless resentment and vengeance are the goals.

The only reasonable option is to move into a post-racial society. We must let go of racial identity and stop seeing each other as racialized collectives. Part of the idea underlying individualism, as opposed to collectivism, is that every person is recognized as a unique individual wholly separate from whatever group they might belong to. That doesn't give them a license to be selfish or disregard community. It means that the individual is seen as just that—an individual. Any attempt to categorize them into collectives based on immutable characteristics will be arbitrary and irrational. Ultimately, we are all mudbloods anyway, right? So, who cares?

The Future

It is clear that we have been conditioned to see and think about race in a certain way in this country. Because of that, it will be undeniably difficult to abandon that lens to view race as the arbitrary fabrication that it is. It seems to me that the best way to do this is to intentionally abandon that collectivist thinking, embrace individualism, and instill these fundamental principles in our children. We must build the next generation to be better than us. That is how we will change the world.

This has been my mission: to help initiate a true paradigm shift in America that sees our society abandon its vile infatuation with racial identity. I believe we must do everything we can to resist, reject, and dismantle the poison of Critical Race Theory. We must work to create a colorblind society and fulfill Dr. King's dream. The words "black" and "white" must be reduced to nothing more than physical descriptors, no different than "blonde" or "brunette." We must reject the idea that these words should carry moral weight or that they be used to assign guilt or victimhood, especially with children. We must, with every fiber of our beings, refuse to raise our children to be victims.

Many believe that our society is too far gone, that the historical wounds are too deep, and that the cancer has too badly metastasized. I refuse to believe that. We have already overcome much in our young history as a nation. I am certain some colonists proclaimed that the Continental Army attempting to defeat the greatest military in the world to earn our independence from England was doomed to be futile. I am sure countless people believed women would never gain the right to vote or be viewed as equals to men. I am aware of many who believed abolishing slavery was well beyond the realm of possibility and that any efforts to do so should be abandoned. There are many such examples of seemingly insurmountable obstacles in our national history—obstacles that tore at the very fabric of our society that were nonetheless ultimately conquered.

Achieving colorblindness will not be done overnight and perhaps, it won't even be achieved in my generation. But the age-old Greek proverb teaches us that a society grows great when old men plant trees under whose shade they know they may never sit. I want to help plant those trees. I hope you will plant them with me. Our country has already been through multiple paradigm shifts that have vastly altered our trajectory. I am thoroughly convinced that we can create another one together.

Afterword

People often ask me, "What can we do? How do we fight the onslaught of Critical Race Theory?" The answer isn't simple and I'm not going to pretend to have all the answers. But I know we must push back in any way we can. Here is some general advice I would give:

Never Apologize to the Mob

The fear of being canceled is real. The threat of being canceled is real. People have lost their jobs, had their reputations destroyed, and had mobs come after them, all for the crime of speaking against progressive dogma. I get it. No one wants that to happen to them. But the absolute worst thing you can possibly do is bow down to the totalitarians and apologize. Never, ever do that. You will not make anything better, and all you will do is empower the mob. As Jordan Peterson often says, when you bow down to a tyrant, you have only succeeded in creating worse tyrants.

For example, a contestant on *The Bachelor* received a ton of back-lash when people discovered she had attended an antebellum party years earlier. When the show's host defended her and asked people to give her some grace, he too, became a target of the mob. Instead of standing their ground, both the contestant and host groveled—but it wasn't enough. The host lost his job and the contestant ended up having to delete her social media accounts because of the abuse being heaped upon her. The cancellation mob consumed them both and then moved on, empowered, to search for new victims.

If you find yourself the target of one of these bullying campaigns, do not back down! Stand your ground and fight back. Bullies only go after people they think are weak—people they think they can bend to their will. The last thing the bully wants or expects is to be punched in the mouth. So that's exactly what you need to do. Punch them in the mouth—figuratively, of course.

Speak the Truth

This isn't all that different from the previous point, but it is extremely important. You know what the truth is. You cannot be afraid to speak it. We are constantly being bombarded with lies and distortions of reality on every sociopolitical topic under the sun, including race. Yes, the truth will offend people. Yes, it will make them angry. But so what? The truth is more important than their feelings. That doesn't mean we set out to purposefully offend people, but it does mean we cannot sacrifice the truth for the sake of their feelings. And make no mistake, there is no such thing as "my truth" or "your truth." There is only *the* truth. There is a saying that I love that goes, "Being offended doesn't mean you're right." That is abso-lutely correct. Being offended means nothing, actually. It tells us nothing about reality or what's true. We can and should speak the truth in love. But what we also need to understand is that no matter what you say or what position you take, somebody somewhere is not going to like it. Someone is going to be offended no matter what. So, you might as well speak the truth.

Reject the Premise

Do not allow the mob to control the narrative. Do not play by its rules or erroneous definitions of words. Reject the premise that progressivism is automatically correct in its assumptions on race. Reject the premise that racism is endemic in our society. Reject the premise that a singular example of perceived racism is evidence of a widespread, systemic problem. Reject the premise that Critical Race Theory is not taught in schools. Reject the premise that only white people can be racist, etc. Do not allow anyone to sidestep these kinds of arguments without challenge. Call out the deceptive tactics they like to use like motte-and-baily, tu quoque, the Kafka trap, etc. Know what they are, and be able to spot them when they are employed. Race activists will attempt to treat their premises as foregone conclusions and build other nonsensical arguments on them. Do not let them.

Reach the Next Generation

Make no mistake, we are in the midst of a culture war, and the other side has absolutely no problem going after children. It's our job to ensure that we reach the next generation before it's too late. Even just raising our own children to embrace the ideals of colorblindness and reject any form of race-centric ideology will go a long way. (We should be doing that anyway, culture war or not.) Additionally, we should take any opportunity we have to mentor children and be sure to promote these values whenever and wherever we can. If you are a teacher, be deliberate about promoting colorblindness in your classroom. If you are a camp counselor, be deliberate about promoting colorblindness in your camp. If you are a coach, be deliberate about promoting colorblindness on your teams. It must be done in schools, in sports, in church, everywhere you go, because you can rest assured that the CRT activists already are doing this every chance they get. We must boldly counter their toxic message and provide the antidote to the next generation before the poison has a chance to take effect. Speak out.

Get Involved in Politics

I'm not saying you have to run for office, but we have to be involved with politics, particularly on the local level. We have already seen the effect parents have had by showing up to school board meetings and making their voices heard. We cannot be passive. We have to keep an eye on what's happening with policy and assertively push back against things that do not align with our values. One reason progressives are so much more effective is because they are better at organizing and protesting. Their ideas are terrible, but they are good at making a miniscule percentage of people seem like a majority. We have to be better at this than they are. The most impact happens at the local level. We must be cultural and political influencers there. If you feel compelled to run for office, please do. We definitely need a lot more good people in government willing to work to actually make a difference.

Remove Them from Positions of Power

Race activists insert themselves anywhere they feel they can have power and influence over others, and they immediately begin pushing their ideology. We must use our voices and advocate for removing them from power anywhere we see the ideology being infused. No more CRT. No more DEI. No more racial-sensitivity training. No more "culturally responsive" teaching. No more. Get them off the school boards. Get them out of classrooms. Get them out of management. Get them out of government. Take away their power.

Trust in God

Ultimately, there is only so much we can do as fallible human beings. Ultimately, we need to just pray, trust in God, and continue to do what we know is right. As the Bible tells us, "Fight the good fight of faith . . . take up the whole armor of God, that you may be able to withstand in the evil day and having done all, to stand" (1 Timothy 6:12, Ephesians 6:13). Ultimately, no matter what ends up happening, God is in control. We can find peace in that fact.

Notes

Chapter 1: What Is Critical Race Theory?

1. Richard Delgado and Jean Stefancic, *Critical Race Theory: An Introduction* (New York: NYU Press, 2017), 3.
2. Staff Writer, "Thomas Sowell Commentary: Equal Treatment Doesn't Guarantee Equal Outcomes," *Columbus Dispatch,* January 4, 2015, https://www.dispatch.com/story/opinion/cartoons/2015/01/05/thomas-sowell-commentary-equal-treatment/23674078007.
3. Laura Italiano, "'Whiteness' Exhibit at Smithsonian's African American History Museum Causes Stir," *New York Post,* July 16, 2020, https://nypost.com/2020/07/16/african-american-history-museums-whiteness-exhibit-raising-eyebrows.
4. Nick Monroe, "The New York Times Downplays Acceleration of Critical Race Theory in Schools," *The Post Millennial,* April 30, 2021, https://thepostmillennial.com/new-york-times-glosses-over-that-push-for-critical-race-theory-in-schools-is-accelerating.
5. Douglas Murray, *The Madness of Crowds: Gender, Race, and Identity* (London: Bloomsbury Continuum, 2019), 7–8.

Chapter 2: Münchausen's by Proxy

1. Julie Gregory, *Sickened: The True Story of a Lost Childhood* (New York: Bantam Books, 2008), 24.
2. Bruce Hopper, *Pan-Sovietism: The Issue Before America and the World* (Boston, Massachusetts: Houghton Mifflin Company, 1931), 87.
3. Jack Schneider and Jennifer Berkshire, "Parents Claim They Have the Right to Shape Their Kids' School Curriculum. They Don't," *Washington Post,* October 21,

2021, https://www.washingtonpost.com/outlook/parents-rights-protests
-kids/2021/10/21/5cf4920a-31d4-11ec-9241-aad8e48f01ff_story.html.

4. Sam Dorman, "Head of Teachers Union Praises Op-Ed Claiming Parents Don't
    Have Right to Shape Kids' Curriculum," Fox News, October 26, 2021, https://
    www.foxnews.com/politics/randi-weingarten-teachers-union-parents-rights-op
    -ed-kids-curriculum.

5. Jessica Chasmar, "Democrats, Teachers Unions Fight to Keep Parents from Learning
    What Their Kids Are Taught," Fox News, February 4, 2022, https://www.
    foxnews.com/politics/democrats-teachers-unions-parents-learning-kids-taught.

6. *Merriam-Webster*, s.v. "race (*n.*)," https://merriam-webster.com/dictionary/race.

7. Charles Dickens, *A Tale of Two Cities* (New York: Cosmopolitan Book Corporation,
    1921), 208.

8. Rebecca Lamason et. al, "SLC24A5, a Putative Cation Exchanger, Affects
    Pigmentation in Zebrafish and Humans," *Science* 310, no. 5755 (December 16,
    2005): 1782–86, https://www.science.org/doi/10.1126/science.1116238.

9. Kenneth Dodge et al., "Hostile Attributional Bias and Aggressive Behavior in Global
    Context," *Psychological and Cognitive Sciences* 112, no. 30 (July 13, 2015): 9310–
    15, https://doi.org/10.1073/pnas.1418572112.

Chapter 3: That's Not CRT!

1. "Teaching Truth to Power: Critical Race Theory Summer School," The African
    American Policy Forum, https://www.aapf.org/crtsummerschool.

2. Selim Algar and Kate Sheehy, "NYC Public School Asks Parents to 'Reflect' on
    Their 'Whiteness,'" *New York Post*, February 16, 2021, nypost.com/2021/02/16/
    nyc-public-school-asks-parents-to-reflect-on-their-whiteness.

3. Laura Meckler, "Can Honors and Regular Students Learn Math Together? A New
    Approach Argues Yes," *Washington Post*, June 4, 2021, https://www.washingtonpost.
    com/education/2021/06/04/california-math-class-detrack-race-equity.

4. "Portland Public Schools Racial Educational Equity Policy," Portland Public
    Schools, https://www.pps.net/cms/lib/OR01913224/Centricity/Domain/4814
    /2.10.010-P.pdf.

5. Meg Woolhouse, "Boston Public Schools Suspends Test for Advanced Learning
    Classes; Concerns about Program's Racial Inequities Linger," GBH News,
    February 26, 2021, https://www.wgbh.org/news/education/2021/02/26/citing
    -racial-inequities-boston-public-schools-suspend-advanced-learning-classes.

6. Michael Lee, "Arizona Education Department Encourages Talking to Babies
    about Racism, Says 3-Month-Olds Can Be Racist," *Washington Examiner*,
    March 4, 2021, https://www.washingtonexaminer.com/news/arizona-education
    -baby-toddler-racism-three-months.

7. Jerry Fingal and Samantha Mack, "10 Resources for Teaching Anti-Racism,"
    ISTE, January 17, 2022, https://www.iste.org/explore/classroom/10-resources
    -teaching-legacy_of_MLK.

8. "The Children's Equity Project," Center for Child and Family Success, Arizona State University, https://childandfamilysuccess.asu.edu/cep.

9. Bill Bush, "Conservative Group Accuses Columbus Schools of Racism Based on a Press Release," *Columbus Dispatch,* May 12, 2021, https://www.dispatch .com/story/news/2021/05/11/parents-defending-educatd-c-conservative-startup -puts-ccs-its-sites-call-racism-investigation-based/5044434001.

10. "Mentor Public Schools' Presentation Explains to Teachers How They Can Become 'Co-Conspirators While Using a Curriculum Rooted in Whiteness,'" Parents Defending Education, https://defendinged.org/incidents/mentor-public-schools-presentation-explains-to-teachers-how-they-can-become-co-conspirators-while-using-a-curriculum-rooted-in-whiteness.

11. Daniel Bergner, "'White Fragility' Is Everywhere. But Does Antiracism Training Work?" *New York Times,* July 15, 2020, https://foxbaltimore.com/news/city-in-crisis/towson-symposium-professors-argue-standard-english-is-racialized-as-white.

12. Rich Lowry, "The War on Gifted-and-Talented Programs," *National Review,* October 12, 2021, https://www.nationalreview.com/2021/10/the-war-on-gifted-and-talented-programs.

Chapter 4: The Motte and the Bailey

1. Passion City Church, "The Beloved Community – Dan Cathy, Lecrae, Louie Giglio," YouTube, June 15, 2020, https://www.youtube.com/watch?v+xEui-03Jcc4.

2. Bill Barajas, "VIDEO: White People Kneel, Ask Forgiveness from the Black Community in Third Ward," Click2Houston, June 1, 2020, https://www .click2houston.com/news/local/2020/06/01/video-white-people-kneel-ask -forgiveness-from-the-black-community-in-third-ward.

3. "ELCA Anti-Racism Pledge," Evangelical Lutheran Church in America, https:// www.elca.org/racialjusticepledge.

4. "Facing Racism: A Vision of the Intercultural Community Churchwide Antiracism Policy," Presbyterian Church, https://facing-racism.pcusa.org.

5. Les Landau, *Star Trek: The Next Generation,* Season 6, Episode 11, Paramount Television, 1992.

6. George Orwell, *Nineteen Eighty-Four* (London: Secker and Warburg, 1949), 249–57.

Chapter 5: Justice and Vengeance

1. Aleksandr Solzhenitsyn, *The Gulag Archipelago* (Paris, France: Éditions du Seuil, 1974), 12–13.

2. Booker T. Washington, *My Larger Education: Being Chapters from My Experience* (New York: Start Publishing, 2013), 39.

3. Sandra Sobieraj Westfall, "Kamala Harris Reacts to Mocking Mispronunciations of Her Name: 'It's about Respect,'" *People,* October 30, 2020, https://people.

com/politics/kamala-harris-reacts-to-mocking-mispronunciations-of-her-name.

4. Neil MacFarquhar, "Murders Spiked in 2020 in Cities across the United States," *New York Times,* September 27, 2021, https://www.nytimes.com/2021/09/27/us/fbi-murders-2020-cities.html.

5. "Expanded Homicide Data Table 6," 2019 FBI Uniform Crime Report, https://ucr.fbi.gov/crime-in-the-u.s/2019/crime-in-the-u.s.-2019/tables/expanded-homicide-data-table-6.xls.

6. Brian Flood, "CNN's Don Lemon Scolds Terry Crews, Says Black Lives Matter Is about Police Brutality, Not Black-on-Black Violence," Fox News, July 7, 2020, https://www.foxnews.com/media/don-lemon-terry-crews-black-lives-matter.

7. Amos Tversky and Daniel Kahneman, "Availability: A Heuristic for Judging Frequency and Probability," *Cognitive Psychology* 5, no. 2 (September 1973): 207–32, https://doi.org/10.1016/0010-0285(73)90033-9.

8. Silvia Foster-Frau et al., "Poll: Black Americans Fear More Racist Attacks after Buffalo Shooting," *Washington Post,* May 21, 2022, https://www.washingtonpost.com/nation/2022/05/21/post-poll-black-americans.

9. "Expanded Homicide Data Table 6."

Chapter 6: Diversity Is Our Strength?

1. Richard E. Lapchick et al., *The 2021 Racial and Gender Report Card: National Basketball Association,* The Institute for Diversity and Ethics in Sport, August 25, 2021, https://www.tidesport.org/_files/ugd/138a69_4b2910360b754662b5f3cb52675d0faf.pdf.

2. *Fisher v. University of TX at Austin,* 570 S. Ct. 297 (2013) (Thomas concurring opinion), https://supreme.justia.com/cases/federal/us/570/297.

3. Ibid.

4. Emma Colton, "ASU Students Found Guilty after Harassing White Students Slam College's Punishment: 'Actually Violent,'" Fox News, January 4, 2022, https://www.foxnews.com/us/asu-students-reprimanded-white-students-multicultural-center-school-openly-discriminated.

5. "2021 College Free Speech Rankings," College Pulse, https://reports.collegepulse.com/college-free-speech-rankings-2021.

6. Tim Meads, "Shooter Kills 10, Wounds Three in Buffalo Grocery Store; Authorities Investigating as Racially Motivated Attack," The Daily Wire, May 14, 2022, https://www.dailywire.com/news/shooter-kills-10-wounds-three-in-buffalo-grocery-store-authorities-investigating-as-racially-motivated-attack.

7. Melissa Klein and Ben Feuerherd, "Accused NYC Subway Shooter Frank James Indicted on Federal Charges," *New York Post,* May 7, 2022, https://nypost.com/2022/05/07/accused-nyc-subway-shooter-frank-james-indicted-by-grand-jury.

8. Dana Kennedy, "'Not Fitting Their Narrative': Waukesha Feels Abandoned after Tragic Parade Attack," *New York Post,* December 13, 2021, https://nypost.com/2021/12/13/why-waukesha-parade-attack-doesnt-fit-media-narrative.

9. Cristina Marcos, "Scalise: Shooting 'Fortified' My View on Gun Rights," *The Hill*, October 3, 2017, https://thehill.com/homenews/house/353714-scalise-shooting-fortified-view-on-gun-rights.

10. Adam Sabes, "Brett Kavanaugh Attempted Murder Suspect Nicholas Roske Pleads Not Guilty," Fox News, June 22, 2022, https://www.foxnews.com/politics/brett-kavanaugh-attempted-murder-suspect-nicholas-roske-pleads-not-guilty.

11. Bradford Richardson, "Liberal Professors Outnumber Conservatives 12 to 1: Study," *Washington Times*, October 6, 2016, https://www.washingtontimes.com/news/2016/oct/6/liberal-professors-outnumber-conservatives-12-1.

12. Lillian Gissen, "Lebron James' 17-Year-Old Son Bronny Is Trolled with Vile Racist Abuse for Taking a White Girl to His High School Prom…," *Daily Mail*, May 19, 2022, https://www.dailymail.co.uk/femail/article-10833483/LeBron-James-17-year-old-son-Bronny-faces-racist-abuse-taking-white-girl-high-school-prom.html.

13. Brandon Gillespie, "NYC Psychiatrist Claims White People Are 'Psychopathic,' Lie to Themselves with False Sense of Identity," Fox News, June 18, 2021, https://www.foxnews.com/media/new-york-city-psychiatrist-white-people-psychopathic-lie-false-sense-identity.

14. Bye Murica! (@SheIsImaniB), "She isn't totally off here…," Twitter, June 17, 2021, 8:06 a.m., https://twitter.com/SheIsImaniB/status/1405497146594451460?s=20&t=NK3iiFGCgUXSmCkdz1z1oQ.

15. Megan Ming Francis, "We Need to Address the Real Roots of Racial Violence," TEDx video, 19:37, March 21, 2016, https://www.ted.com/talks/megan_ming_francis_we_need_to_address_the_real_roots_of_racial_violence?language=en.

Chapter 7: Inclusion and Compassion, but Not for You

1. Jeanine Tesori and David Lindsay-Abaire, *Shrek the Musical*, 2008.

2. Essential Truth, "Jordan Peterson: The Problem of Too Much Empathy," YouTube, June 26, 2017, https://www.youtube.com/watch?v=sWbj-2DRLps.

3. *Finding Nemo*, directed by Andrew Stanton and Lee Unkrich (Buena Vista Pictures, 2003).

4. Martin Seligman and Steven Maier, "Failure to Escape Traumatic Shock," *Journal of Experimental Psychology* 74, no. 1 (May 1967): 1–9, https://doi.org/10.1037/h0024514.

5. *Avengers: Infinity War*, directed by Joe Russo and Anthony Russo (Walt Disney Studios Motion Pictures, 2018).

6. *Avatar: The Last Airbender*, created by Michael DiMartino and Bryan Konietzko, aired February 21, 2005, on Nickelodeon.

7. J. K. Rowling, *Harry Potter and the Deathly Hallows* (New York: Arthur A. Levine Books, 2007), 296.

8. J. K. Rowling, *Harry Potter and the Order of the Phoenix* (New York: Arthur A. Levine Books, 2003), 687–88.

9. *Star Wars Episode III: Revenge of the Sith*, directed by George Lucas (20th Century Fox, 2013).

10. Alain Boublil and Claude Michel-Schönberg, *Les Misérables: A Musical* (London: Alain Boublil Music, 1998).

11. Thomas Sowell, "Random Thoughts," Jewish World Review, February 1, 2002, https://jewishworldreview.com/cols/sowell050316.php3.

12. George Orwell, *Nineteen Eighty-Four* (London: Secker and Warburg, 1949), 214.

Chapter 8: Equity Is the Opposite of Equality

1. Ayn Rand, *The Return of the Primitive: The Anti-Industrial Revolution* (New York: Meridian, 1999), 144.

2. Kurt Vonnegut, *Harrison Bergeron* (Mercury Press, 1962), 1–6.

3. Selim Algar, "NYC Wants Schools to Rethink Honor Rolls Deemed 'Detrimental' to Students Not Making Grade," *New York Post*, August 31, 2021, https://nypost.com/2021/08/31/nyc-wants-schools-to-rethink-honor-rolls-deemed-detrimental.

4. Ayn Rand, *Philosophy: Who Needs It* (New York: Signet, 1984), 121.

5. Lynn Ahrens and Stephen Flaherty, *Anastasia: The Musical*, 2017.

6. *Major Payne*, directed by Nick Castle (Universal Pictures, 1995).

7. Milton Friedman and Rose Friedman, *Free to Choose: A Personal Statement* (Boston, Massachusetts: Mariner Books, 1990), 148.

Chapter 9: Do Disparities Equal Bias?

1. J. K. Rowling, *Harry Potter and the Order of the Phoenix* (New York: Arthur A. Levine Books, 2003), 319.

2. J. K. Rowling, *Harry Potter and the Deathly Hallows* (New York: Arthur A. Levine Books, 2007), 212.

3. "QuickFacts," United States Census Bureau, https://www.census.gov/quickfacts/fact/table/US/PST045221.

4. "Income, Poverty, and Health Insurance Coverage in the United States: 2020," United States Census Bureau, September 14, 2021, https://www.census.gov/newsroom/press-releases/2021/income-poverty-health-insurance-coverage.html.

5. Nicki Lisa Cole, "What Is Cultural Hegemony?," ThoughtCo., January 5, 2020, https://www.thoughtco.com/cultural-hegemony-3026121.

6. Kevin McCaffree and Anondah Saide, "How Informed Are Americans about Race and Policing?," Skeptic Research Center, February 20, 2021, https://www.skeptic.com/research-center/reports/Research-Report-CUPES-007.pdf.

7. "Fatal Force," *Washington Post*, https://www.washingtonpost.com/graphics/investigations/police-shootings-database/.

8. Ibid.

9. "Table 43: Arrests," 2019 FBI Uniform Crime Report, https://ucr.fbi.gov/crime-in-the-u.s/2019/crime-in-the-u.s.-2019/tables/table-43.

10. Ibid.

11. Heather Mac Donald, *The War on Cops* (New York: Encounter Books, 2016), 38.

12. "Fatal Force."

13. "Table 29: Estimated Number of Arrests," 2019 FBI Uniform Crime Report, https://ucr.fbi.gov/crime-in-the-u.s/2019/crime-in-the-u.s.-2019/tables/table-29.

14. "Table 42: Arrests by Sex," 2019 FBI Uniform Crime Report, https://ucr.fbi.gov/crime-in-the-u.s/2019/crime-in-the-u.s.-2019/topic-pages/tables/table-42.

15. "Fatal Force."

16. Dale Russell, "Young Accused Killer of 6-Month-Old in NW Atlanta in and out of Jail for Years," Fox Atlanta, February 16, 2022, https://www.fox5atlanta.com/news/young-accused-killer-of-six-month-old-in-and-out-of-jail-for-years.

17. "Suspect in Child's Murder Was Out on Bond for Aggravated Robbery," ABC 13, February 19, 2022, https://abc13.com/11-year-old-shot-and-killed-daveyonne-howard-darius-dugas-childs-murder/11577749.

18. Jesse Bunch, "Search Continues for Suspect in Toddler's Downtown Shooting Death," *Pittsburgh Post-Gazette*, May 31, 2022, https://www.post-gazette.com/news/crime-courts/2022/05/31/search-suspect-in-1-year-old-shooting-death-downtown-pittsburgh-markez-anger-londell-falconer/stories/202205310095.

19. Leonydus Johnson (@LeonydusJohnson), "I'm starting a new thread for this year...," Twitter, April 22, 2021, 9:57 a.m., https://twitter.com/LeonydusJohnson/status/1385231216379584512.

20. Leonydus Johnson (@LeonydusJohnson), "I know these are tough to look at...," Twitter, September 4, 2020, 3:02 p.m., https://twitter.com/LeonydusJohnson/status/1301958840024469505.

21. Andy Grimm, "Half of Murder Cases Considered 'Solved' by Chicago Police in 2021 Didn't Lead to Charges," *Chicago Sun-Times*, March 31, 2022, https://chicago.suntimes.com/crime/2022/3/31/22996487/cpd-police-department-clearance-murder-solved-rate-david-brown-kim-foxx-prosecutor-charges.

22. E. Ann Carson, "Prisoners in 2020 – Statistical Tables," Bureau of Justice Statistics, U.S. Department of Justice, December 2021, https://bjs.ojp.gov/content/pub/pdf/p20st.pdf.

23. "Drowning Facts," Centers for Disease Control and Prevention, https://www.cdc.gov/drowning/facts/index.html.

24. "The Father Absence Crisis in America," National Fatherhood Initiative, https://cdn2.hubspot.net/hubfs/135704/NFIFatherAbsenceInfoGraphic071118.pdf.

25. Joseph Chamie, "Out-of-Wedlock Births Rise Worldwide," Yale Global Online, March 16, 2017, https://archive-yaleglobal.yale.edu/content/out-wedlock-births-rise-worldwide.

Chapter 10: The Demand for Racism

1. Patrick Reilly, "Black Woman Accused of Posing as KKK Member, Leaving Threatening Notes for Neighbors," *New York Post*, October 3, 2021, https://nypost.com/2021/10/03/black-woman-accused-of-posing-as-kkk-rep-threatening-neighbors.

2. Steve Rundio, "Viterbo Student Faces Charge for Residence Hall Fire," *La Crosse Tribune*, June 16, 2021, https://lacrossetribune.com/news/local/crime

-and-courts/viterbo-student-faces-charge-for-residence-hall-fire/article
_91b72191-d5fc-55a0-aa2d-08d8ebacc9db.html.

3. Josh Verges, "Racist Threats in White Bear Lake Were a 'Hoax' to Call Attention to Racist Incidents at High School, Officials Say," *Pioneer Press*, April 14, 2021, https://www.twincities.com/2021/04/14/racist-threats-in-white-bear-lake-were-a-hoax-to-call-attention-to-racist-incidents-at-high-school-officials-say.

4. Fox 5 Digital Team, "Former Emory Employee Charged in Racist Graffiti Investigation," Fox 5 Atlanta, September 23, 2021, https://www.fox5atlanta.com/news/former-emory-employee-charged-in-racist-graffiti-investigation.

5. Robert Patrick, "Student Charged with Faking Racist Incident at SIUE," *St. Louis Post-Dispatch*, February 4, 2022, https://www.stltoday.com/news/local/crime-and-courts/student-charged-with-faking-racist-incident-at-siue/article_ce34b603-745f-5cfe-a3db-8cee2afd0a7d.html.

6. Eric Escalante and Jay Kim, "SCUSD Says a Student Was Responsible for Racist Language Written above Drinking Fountains at McClatchy High School," ABC 10, February 17, 2022, https://www.abc10.com/article/news/local/sacramento/sacramento-schools-racism/103-50e59c91-400b-413f-9ca9-2ea0c7f8eefc.

7. Wilfred Reilly, *Hate Crime Hoax* (Washington, D.C.: Regnery Publishing, 2019).

8. Fake Hate Crimes: A Database of Hate Crime Hoaxes in the USA, https://fakehatecrimes.org.

9. Sue Obeidi and Evelyn Alsultany, "'Dune' Repeats Tired Tropes of a White Savior in a Middle Eastern Setting," The Wrap, February 23, 2022, https://www.thewrap.com/dune-tired-tropes-white-savior-middle-east-muslim.

10. Jen Yamato, "At Netflix, 'Cobra Kai' Broke Out. Now Its Whiteness Is under a New Spotlight," *Los Angeles Times*, January 8, 2021, https://www.latimes.com/entertainment-arts/tv/story/2021-01-08/netflix-cobra-kai-season-3-diversity.

11. Tommy Gilligan, "Ex-Twin Josh Donaldson Embroiled in Racism Controversy for Jackie Robinson Comment," *Sports Illustrated*, May 22, 2022, https://www.si.com/fannation/bringmethesports/twins/ex-twin-josh-donaldson-embroiled-in-racism-controversy-for-jackie-robinson-comment.

12. Ken Belson, "Raiders Coach Made Racist Comment about N.F.L. Players' Union Chief," *New York Times*, October 8, 2021, https://www.nytimes.com/2021/10/08/sports/football/nfl-demaurice-smith-jon-gruden-racist-comment.html.

13. Tiffany Hsu, "Aunt Jemima Brand to Change Name and Image over 'Racial Stereotype,'" *New York Times*, June 17, 2020, https://www.nytimes.com/2020/06/17/business/media/aunt-jemima-racial-stereotype.html.

14. Brakkton Booker, "Uncle Ben's Changing Name to Ben's Original after Criticism of Racial Stereotyping," NPR, September 23, 2020, https://www.npr.org/sections/live-updates-protests-for-racial-justice/2020/09/23/916012582/uncle-bens-changing-name-to-bens-original-after-criticism-of-racial-stereotyping.

15. Darryl Fears, "The Racist Legacy Many Birds Carry: Birders Grapple with Complicated Past linked to Slavery, White Supremacy," *Washington Post*, June 3, 2021, https://www.washingtonpost.com/climate-environment/interactive/2021/bird-names-racism-audubon/.

16. Margaret Sanger, "Apostle of Birth Control Sees Cause Gaining Here; Hearing in Albany on Bill to Legalize Practice a Milestone in Long Fight of Margaret Sanger—Even China Awakening to Need of Selective Methods, She Says," *New York Times,* April 8, 1923, https://www.nytimes.com/1923/04/08/archives/apostle-of-birth-control-sees-cause-gaining-here-hearing-in-albany.html.

17. "Letter from Margaret Sanger to Dr. C. J. Gamble, December 10, 1939," Margaret Sanger Papers, Sophia Smith Collection, Smith College Libraries, https://libex.smith.edu/omeka/items/show/495.

18. Alexis McGill Johnson, "I'm the Head of Planned Parenthood. We're Done Making Excuses for Our Founder," *New York Times,* April 17, 2021, https://www.nytimes.com/2021/04/17/opinion/planned-parenthood-margaret-sanger.html.

19. James Studnicki, John W. Fisher, and James L. Sherley, "Perceiving and Addressing the Pervasive Racial Disparity in Abortion," *Health Services Research and Managerial Epidemiology* 7 (August 18, 2020), https://doi.org/10.1177/2333392820949743.

20. "Reproductive Justice Resources from a Staten Island Organizer," Planned Parenthood of Greater New York, https://www.plannedparenthood.org/planned-parenthood-greater-new-york/campaigns/reproductive-justice-and-staten-island.

21. "Black Organizing," Planned Parenthood of South, East and North Florida, https://www.plannedparenthood.org/planned-parenthood-south-east-north-florida/action-center/black-organizing.

22. "Anti-Racism Resources," Planned Parenthood of Southwestern Oregon, https://www.plannedparenthood.org/planned-parenthood-southwestern-oregon/anti-racism-resources.

23. "Planned Parenthood of the Pacific Southwest's Commitment to Black Communities," Planned Parenthood of the Pacific Southwest, https://www.plannedparenthood.org/planned-parenthood-pacific-southwest/campaigns/race-equity.

24. "Planned Parenthood Southwestern Oregon Board Supports the Movement for Black Lives," Planned Parenthood of Southwestern Oregon, https://www.plannedparenthood.org/planned-parenthood-southwestern-oregon/supporting-black-lives-matter-movement.

25. Lynn Elber and Mark Kennedy, "NBC Cancels Megyn Kelly's Show after Blackface Controversy," Associated Press, October 26, 2018, https://apnews.com/article/entertainment-north-america-megyn-kelly-tv-ap-top-news-a84a7250b109411591ed6b976be800a0.

26. Shelby Steele, *White Guilt* (New York: HarperCollins, 2009), 368.

Chapter 11: Up from Slavery

1. Thomas Sowell, *Discrimination and Disparities* (New York: Basic Books, 2011).

2. Booker T. Washington, *Up from Slavery* (New York: Simon and Schuster, 1901), 23.

3. Ron Haskins, "Three Simple Rules Poor Teens Should Follow to Join the Middle Class," Brookings Institution, March 13, 2013, https://www.brookings.edu/opinions/three-simple-rules-poor-teens-should-follow-to-join-the-middle-class.

4. Thomas Sowell, *The Thomas Sowell Reader* (New York: Basic Books, 2011), 13.
5. Michael P. Johnson and James L. Roark, *Black Masters: A Free Family of Color in the Old South* (New York: Norton, 1984), 14.
6. John P. McKay et al., *A History of World Societies* (Boston, Massachusetts: Bedford/St. Martin's, 2009), 846.
7. "Booker T. Washington High School," Public School Review, https://www.publicschoolreview.com/booker-t-washington-high-school-profile.
8. "Booker T. Washington High School," Public School Review, https://www.publicschoolreview.com/booker-t-washington-high-school-profile/30314.
9. "Booker T. Washington High School," Public School Review, https://www.publicschoolreview.com/booker-t-washington-middle-school-profile/21217.
10. "Baltimore City Public Schools School District," Public School Review, https://www.publicschoolreview.com/maryland/baltimore-city-public-schools-school-district/2400090-school-district.
11. "6-Year Graduation Rates at Many HBCUs Lower than 20 Percent," *Atlanta Journal-Constitution,* January 29, 2018, https://www.ajc.com/news/local/year-graduation-rates-many-hbcus-lower-than-percent/TH1IXkSReeQEFQnnMjbxQN.
12. "The National Study of Millionaires," Ramsey Solutions, https://www.ramseysolutions.com/retirement/the-national-study-of-millionaires-research.

Chapter 12: The American Cultural Revolution

1. Mao Zedong, *Quotations from Chairman Mao Tse-Tung* (China Books, 1972), 33.
2. *Encyclopedia Britannica,* s.v. "critical theory," https://www.britannica.com/topic/critical-theory.
3. "Resisting Critical Race Theory Workshop: All Sessions," New Discourses, March 25, 2022, https://newdiscourses.com/2022/03/resisting-critical-race-theory-workshop-all-sessions.
4. Robin DiAngelo and Özlem Sensoy, *Is Everyone Really Equal?: An Introduction to Key Concepts in Social Justice Education* (New York: Teachers College Press, 2011), 5.
5. *Fresh Air,* "Newly Released Documents Detail Traumas of China's Cultural Revolution," hosted by Terry Gross, aired on May 5, 2016, on NPR, https://www.npr.org/2016/05/05/476873854/newly-released-documents-detail-traumas-of-chinas-cultural-revolution.
6. C. S. Lewis, *God in the Dock: Essays on Theology and Ethics* (New York: HarperOne, 2014), 292.

Chapter 13: Gratitude and Perspective

1. Maharishi International University, "Jim Carrey at MIU: Commencement Address at the 2014 Graduation," YouTube, May 30, 2014, https://www.youtube.com/watch?v=V80-gPkpH6M.

2. Tim Lott, "Jordan Peterson: 'The Pursuit of Happiness Is a Pointless Goal,'" *The Guardian*, January 21, 2018, https://www.theguardian.com/global/2018/jan/21/jordan-peterson-self-help-author-12-steps-interview.

3. *The Legend of Korra*, season 2, episode 10, "A New Spiritual Age," directed by Ian Graham, aired November 8, 2013, on Nickelodeon.

4. Martin Seligman, *Learned Optimism* (Boston, Massachusetts: Nicholas Brealey Publishing, 2018).

5. Hugo Gye, "America IS the 1%. You Need Just $34,000 Annual Income to Be in the Global Elite…and HALF the World's Richest People Live in the U.S.," Daily Mail, January 5, 2012, https://www.dailymail.co.uk/news/article-2082385/We-1—You-need-34k-income-global-elite—half-worlds-richest-live-U-S.html.

Chapter 14: Colorblindness vs. CRT

1. Founders Ministries, "Ethnic Gnosticism – Dr. Voddie Baucham," YouTube, March 28, 2019, https://www.youtube.com/watch?v=Ip3nV6S_fYU.

2. Upton Sinclair, *I, Candidate for Governor: And How I Got Licked* (Berkeley, California: University of California Press, 1994), 109.